GRC
THROUGH
JOY

Shepherd Hoodwin

Summerjoy Press
LAGUNA NIGUEL, CALIFORNIA

GROWING THROUGH JOY

Summerjoy Press
99 Pearl
Laguna Niguel CA 92677-4818

shoodwin@gmail.com
https://shepherdhoodwin.com

Copyright © 2015, 2020 by Shepherd Hoodwin

All rights reserved. No part of this publication may be reproduced, stored in a retrieval system, or transmitted, in any form or by any means, electronic, mechanical, photocopying, recording, or otherwise, without the prior written permission of the publisher, except by a reviewer, who may quote brief passages in a review.

ISBN: 9798651017300; Kindle: 9781885469175

Photograph of Shepherd Hoodwin by John Kilis.

Dedicated to

Susannah Redelfs

ACKNOWLEDGMENTS

My clients, for their questions and the use of session material.

Leslie-Anne Skolnik, Stan Grindstaff, Ellen Fauerbach, Dave Gregg, and Pat Kendall, for editing.

Linda Scheurle, Fay Goldie, Seth Cohn, Kent Babcock, and Patricia Englert, for transcribing.

CONTENTS

ACKNOWLEDGMENTS _____iv

PREFACE _____x
   MICHAEL CHANNELING _____x
   ORGANIZATION _____xi
   EDITING _____xi

INTRODUCTION _____xiii

I GROWING CONSCIOUSLY _____1

1 ❀ CULTIVATING THE HABIT OF HAPPINESS _____2

2 ❀ GROWTH _____8

3 ❀ GROWTH WITH AWARENESS _____12

4 ❀ THE SPEED OF GROWTH _____16

5 ❀ EVOLUTION THROUGH CREATIVE PLAY _____18

6 ❀ JOY _____27

II ESSENCE AND GUIDES _____34

7 ❀ ESSENCE _____35
   WHAT IS YOUR ESSENCE? _____35
   ESSENCE BOREDOM _____36
   INTEGRATING WITH YOUR ESSENCE _____36
   ESSENCE CONTACT _____37
   THE BIG PICTURE _____38
   INITIATIVE _____38
   IDENTITY _____38
   LIKE PARENTS AND CHILD _____40
   THE COMING FORTH OF YOUR ESSENCE _____42
   THE TECHNICOLOR SELF _____43

8 ❀ WORKING WITH SPIRIT GUIDES _____45

III SPIRITUALITY 58

9 ❋ THE LARGER VIEW 59
   A FOUNTAINHEAD 59
   UNIVERSAL ENERGY 59
   REALITY 59
   WORDS 59
   SEEKING 59

10 ❋ LIFE COURSE 61
   DESTINY 61
   FREE WILL 62
   THE VALUE OF ACKNOWLEDGMENT 62
   WHERE TO LIVE 63
   NAMES 63

11 ❋ NEW AGE MODALITIES 65
   RIGHT FOR YOU 65
   MEDITATION 65
   OUT-OF-BODY EXPERIENCES 66
   DREAMS 66
   PYRAMIDS 66
   CREATIVE VISUALIZATION 66
   AFFIRMATIONS 67

12 ❋ MASTERY 69
   THE UNIVERSE-ITY 69
   BEING UNLIMITED 69
   THE TRUTH 69
   KNOWLEDGE 69
   SELF-UNDERSTANDING 70
   CHANGING YOUR BELIEFS 70
   MAINTAINING SPIRITUAL MOVEMENT 71
   THE SPIRITUAL PATH 72
   COMFORT IN THE BODY 73
   SUFFERING 74
   CRISES 74
   UNPLEASANTNESS 74
   BUSY-MINDEDNESS 74
   ASKING 75
   BEING SPIRIT-FULL 75
   COMPLETING THE PHYSICAL PLANE 75

CONTENTS

IV PERSPECTIVES ON SELF — 77

13 ❈ THE BEAUTIFUL SELF — 78
- NEEDS — 78
- PERFECTION — 78
- APPRECIATION — 78

14 ❈ A HOUSE DIVIDED — 79
- PURE EMOTION — 79
- SAFETY — 79
- SELF-JUDGMENT — 79
- FALSE HUMILITY — 80
- COMPARISONS — 80
- MASTERING DUALITY — 82
- AVOIDANCE — 83
- GUILT — 83
- WANTING — 84

15 ❈ HANDLING DIFFICULT EMOTIONS — 85
- NAMING PAIN — 85
- A GREAT OPPORTUNITY — 85
- FEAR — 85
- DOUBT — 89
- ANGER — 89
- HATE — 95
- RELEASE — 96
- PRIMING THE PUMP — 96
- LAYERS OF EMOTIONS — 97
- VALUING EMOTIONS — 99
- DETACHING FROM FEELINGS — 100
- WHATEVER YOU ARE FEELING — 100
- BALANCE — 100

16 ❈ WORKING WITH YOURSELF — 102
- FINDING YOURSELF — 102
- GENERATING CLARITY — 102
- CHANGING YOUR LIFE — 103
- TO SOMEONE SEVENTY-FIVE YEARS OLD — 104

17 ❈ CHOICES — 105
- LESSONS — 105
- PRIORITIES — 105

DECISIONS	105
SOLUTIONS	106
KEEP IT MOVING	106

18 ❁ ACHIEVEMENT — 107
ACCOMPLISHMENTS	107
MOVEMENT	107
OBSTACLES	107
TRY AND TRY AGAIN?	107
EXPERIMENTS	108

19 ❁ AFFIRMING LIFE — 109
THE MEANING OF LIFE	109
SUICIDE	109
TO SOMEONE CONSIDERING SUICIDE	109
COMFORT	111
THE PURSUIT OF JOY	112
SPONTANEITY	112
BEING CAREFREE	113
HAPPINESS	113
A LIGHTER VIEW	114
ENJOYMENT	114
KNOWING	115

V FOLLOWING THE PATH — 116

20 ❁ TRANSCENDENCE AND SELF-KNOWLEDGE — 117

21 ❁ INTEGRATION THROUGH THE HEART — 123

22 ❁ ACCEPTANCE AND TAKING ACTION — 127

23 ❁ OPENING TO WHOLENESS — 131

VI PRESENT IN THE NOW — 135

24 ❁ SILENCE—THE GREAT MOTHER — 136

25 ❁ RELEASING FEAR OF THE CURRENT

CONTENTS

INSTANT _____ 137

26 ✹ ENGAGING WITH THE UNIQUENESS OF EACH MOMENT_____ 143

BACK MATTER_____ **150**

ABOUT THE AUTHOR _____ 151

GLOSSARY _____ 153

OTHER BOOKS BY SHEPHERD HOODWIN _____ 154

REVIEWS _____ 158

PREFACE

The spiritual path is a journey into joy. In joy, life flows freely in us and we flow freely in life. We do not learn to live in joy overnight; it is a lifelong process. Joy is not found merely by smiling and thinking positive thoughts, but by releasing our blocks and opening, a step at a time, to our soul.

Pain is a message that something is wrong. We can grow by constructively dealing with it, but when we live with consciousness and skill, we minimize pain and increasingly grow through joyful means rather than the "school of hard knocks."

I accessed the material in this book through channeling, working with a nonphysical entity known as Michael. Before reading it, you might find some background helpful.

MICHAEL CHANNELING

Channeling is a process of allowing a nonphysical intelligence to express through a person who is the "channel." It can be in words, energy, emotion, movement, and/or music, among other things. Michael is the name of a group or "entity" of 1,050 individual souls who have completed the physical and astral planes of creation, and teach from the causal plane. This is why they refer to themselves as "we." (They are not the same as the archangel Michael.) There are several Michael books by a number of other channels and authors who work with this same Michael group.

Most of the other Michael books deal with the Michael teachings, a complex and fascinating body of information about the way we set up our lives. *Journey of Your Soul: A Channel Explores the Michael Teachings* is my contribution thus far to that body of information. *Growing Through Joy*, like *Loving from Your Soul* and the other books in this series, does not cover the technical aspects of the Michael teachings, although it illuminates many of its principles. The few terms associated with the teachings are defined in the glossary.

ORGANIZATION

More than half the material in this book comes from lectures. The rest is from individual sessions. Some of the chapters are compilations of passages from various lectures and individual sessions. Most of those passages are in their own subchapter. If there are two or more different passages in a single subchapter, they are separated by asterisks. Questions and comments are italicized. Some chapters contain material that was originally directed to a specific person, yet is potentially useful to others. Unless implied by subtitles or questions, these are noted under the chapter title: *To a Specific Individual*, etc.

EDITING

When I channel, Michael makes use of the contents of my consciousness, and to some degree is limited by my limitations. Although this material is well beyond what I could produce on my own, it is also mine, and I take full responsibility for it. In general, I treated the original transcripts like first drafts, and polished them as I would my own writing, cutting, rearranging, and rewriting as necessary. Before publication I channeled Michael to get their modifications and "stamp of approval."

Growing Through Joy presupposes we each are a soul who has lived other lives, but believing in reincarnation or even in channeling is not necessary for an enjoyable and profitable reading of it. You can validate most of the ideas in it for yourself, and Michael encourages you to do so.

Sessions with Michael are themselves experiences of growing through joy. May you experience this as you read their words.

Shepherd Hoodwin
Laguna Niguel, California

June 15, 2020

INTRODUCTION

To grow through joy is to live gently and wisely without rigidity. To grow through pain is to live forcibly and unconsciously without peace. Each person is growing, one way or the other.

This book is a collection of addresses and counseling we have given through this channel about the spiritual path and its implications. We hope that you find in it insights that support you on your path and assist you in growing through joy.

Our love is with you as a friend along the way.

    Michael

Part I

GROWING CONSCIOUSLY

1 ❈ CULTIVATING THE HABIT OF HAPPINESS

Many people feel that happiness is unattainable for them, at least with the way things are now. It is often assumed that it will become more possible in the future when they have grown, healed, released, or learned more, or when they have changed their circumstances, such as by becoming rich, finding a mate, or dumping a mate, as the case may be. We would like to propose that, at least partly, being happy is a habit—a habit in the way you approach your life—that can be learned, now, just the way things are for you.

It is really not that difficult to be happy. When you were a young child, you probably had a fairly unencumbered capacity for happiness, but you lacked the conscious skills necessary to maintain it consistently; your happiness largely depended upon your needs being met by those around you. We are not suggesting that you go back to the state you were in as a child in order to be happy, but that you move forward into the expanded happiness possible to an adult that is not dependent on outer circumstances.

There are activities that feel especially good to you. These might include, for example, singing, making art, having sex, dancing, doing hard physical work, and taking walks. Part of happiness is regularly including in your life as many of them as you can, making them priorities. If you do not particularly enjoy doing, say, domestic chores, you might pay someone else to do them who presumably does enjoy doing them. On the other hand, it is an interesting spiritual challenge to find a way to have fun while doing them. Happiness is more than doing the things that make it easy for you to feel good, because obviously, life is not made up only of those things; happiness is also finding ways to enjoy whatever you do, bringing forth joy from within. A hearty sense of humor can be very helpful in this.

CULTIVATING THE HABIT OF HAPPINESS

The biggest obstacle to being happy is taking problems too seriously, however you define your problems. There are those who remain relatively happy in the midst of dire circumstances, such as major illness, and others who can be caused to be unhappy over relatively minor things. If you or someone you love is dying of a painful disease, obviously you are not going to be happy about that. But when you have the habit of being happy, your happiness is no longer so much about circumstances, but about the free expression of your spirit into your life.

Meeting challenges such as a major illness can ultimately expand your capacity for happiness. It is not the case that your essence puts you through hellish experiences in order to expand your capacity for happiness. On the physical plane, you do sometimes go through hell but not because your essence insists on it. Sometimes you or someone close to you insists on it. Sometimes "stuff happens"—you encounter some of the hazards inherent in the physical plane. Sometimes you choose to be in a hellish circumstance to be of service to others, to reach out and bring joy where it is deeply needed. However, if in the process, you forget your own joy, it is like being a carpenter who arrives at a building site having left his hammer and nails at home—there is some useful work he can do, but not as much as if he had all the necessary tools.

You can experience happiness even when you feel sadness, grief, anxiety, or fear. Happiness is not being in denial of what you feel, but being at peace with it. If you are in the habit of being happy, you do not need to be in denial of anything, partly because you do not take problems too seriously. You give them their due, taking care of what needs to be taken care of, loving and nurturing yourself and others. However, you do not succumb to the illusion that those things are the totality of reality. You have perspective on them. As you extend happiness into your "negative" feelings, they can heal, whereas if you dramatize or give excess weight to them, they tend to become stuck.

The point is not to sugarcoat your view of the world but to truly see the world and yourself. If one "wrong" thing dominates your view, you are not seeing the whole. You are seeing a small piece of it, out of proportion. That piece may be important at the moment if it is what you are concentrating on resolving or healing. You would not belittle it or whatever feelings are coming up in you in relationship to it. In happiness, you can appropriately express those feelings—they are energies seeking movement, so you let them move safely without overemphasizing their importance. You do what needs to be done in regard to them, and you see the whole. You know that letting the energy of your feelings move appropriately increases your sense of well-being, and therefore, your happiness.

There are always problems in life—no human being is without them. If you were a mathematician and had no problems to solve, where would you be? You would have to take up a different profession. All the problems have been solved—no more work to do! Mathematicians generally think that solving problems is fun; otherwise, they would not take up that field. Perhaps you like to solve crossword puzzles; a crossword puzzle is a problem, full of unanswered questions. Why would anyone willingly take on another problem? "Oh, I have all these words to find; it's such a burden!" No, people generally think it is fun to solve crossword puzzles, and solving life's problems can likewise be fun. You attempt to solve problems by making choices. As in a game of chess, you can consider the ramifications of your choices: "If I make this move, such-and-such might happen, but if I make that one, something else might happen."

If you think that your individual choices are more important than they are, you are likely to be tense and will probably not play the game of life with as much fun or perspective. The game is important; otherwise you would not have taken the trouble to have started it. Every choice

CULTIVATING THE HABIT OF HAPPINESS

you make is, on the one hand, vital, but on the other, just one of an infinite number of choices you make. If the results of this present choice do not turn out to be to your liking, you have plenty more choices to make. You may as well make the best choices you can, the ones you will be happiest with. But if you are cultivating the happiness habit, you are pretty happy anyway. You can laugh about what occurs—maybe even as you are crying—and then move on.

Making skillful choices requires clear perspective on the situations with which you are dealing. Those in the habit of being happy can usually find that perspective. However, most people are not yet able to provide perspective for themselves in every situation. It can therefore be useful sometimes to work with someone else—perhaps a therapist or friend—who can see what you are experiencing with more perspective. This can help you develop your own ability to find perspective, so that you do not become dependent on others for it.

Some people think it would be boring to be happy all the time. Happiness is not unrelenting cheerfulness—that *would* be boring. A variety of emotions is part of the spice of life. Sometimes it can make you happy to be forceful if that is the way your energy needs to move. Happiness is not so much a "positive attitude" as much as it is freedom: freedom of self-expression, freedom to be all you are, the knowledge that "I can." Often "I can" does not feel like the truth when it is, and thoughts such as "I shouldn't," "I can't," and "I don't" seem true when they are not. The truth sets you free; believing falsehoods confines you and can cause pain.

There are many ways in which people defeat their own natural urges to happiness. Urges to be more creative or to express yourself, urges to practice a new skill such as playing a musical instrument, and urges to go more deeply within or to reach out to others, are examples of urges to happiness that are often suppressed out of fear—the fear of making a fool of yourself, the fear of what you might find within yourself, or the fear of the rejection by others. Obviously, being happy requires that you allow yourself to move with your urges to happiness, facing your fears with courage. If it is your urge to let loose and be spontaneous, you might do well to get some large sheets of paper and some finger paints, and make wild splashes of color with your hands, or even with your whole body. You might play some expressive music and dance, moving your whole body with freedom and abandon. If you accurately follow your urges to happiness, you will increasingly be happy.

Your path to happiness is your own. When happiness is discussed, those who are not particularly happy may feel left out or even resentful that that is not their experience. Whatever you experience in this or in any other moment is for a good reason, and you have to start where you are. By consciously and lovingly being with that experience, listening and opening to yourself in the midst of it, you will move toward greater happiness. Sometimes, to find happiness, it is necessary to fully experience your unhappiness first, especially if you have been out of touch with your unhappiness. Someone who has been pretending to be happy may feel keenly unhappy when she begins to consider the true nature of happiness. It is true that you can open to happiness right now, just as things are—you can be happy in the midst of unhappy feelings. However, that might be a relatively limited experience of happiness compared to what is possible. If that is the case, enjoy that limited experience, and the experience will grow.

MEDITATION

Let your mind be still. Feel the natural movement of your energy and relax into it. Feel how it is bringing you to expanded openness, deeper feeling, larger perspective, and greater happiness. There is nothing to strive for or struggle with. There is only this moment, now, to be in, expressing the joy of your essence and the freedom of fully being who you are.

Notice around you a beautiful light protecting the open door to the fullness of yourself. Know that nothing can ever close that door for you. Know that you have all you need to learn more happiness skills and that you cannot fail.

You are allowed to be happy. Remember those wise words, "Don't worry, be happy!"

2 ❂ GROWTH

Growth occurs in two parts. The first part, and this is the lion's share of it, is having experience—joyful, painful, or in-between. The second part is coming to know what it is that you experienced—its meaning. All experience can contribute to growth, because all experience is at least somewhat new.

Sometimes you have many lifetimes in a row that are busy and full of events. You are experiencing at least the first part of growth. After a while, you may find it necessary to have a lifetime or two that are quieter and more devoted to the second part of growth, contemplating the meaning of your experiences. You may not be aware that this is what you are doing, but in such a life, you are not bored; you feel the big meal in your stomach slowly digesting, so to speak. When it is all digested, you feel hungry for new experiences and become more active again. The cycle of growth moves on.

This is similar to what occurs in physical growth. A child may quickly grow four inches, not grow further for a year, and then shoot up three more inches. That apparently inactive year is as much a part of his growth process as the months when measurable growth occurs. During it, he assimilates the previous changes in his body, learning to live and move in new ways, and prepares for the further changes to come.

If you feel that you are growing more slowly than you would like, perhaps you have too many unresolved past experiences to take in new ones. If that is the case, growth for you is represented more by its second part, assimilation.

Both joyful and painful experiences need to be understood and assimilated. Exploring and completing joyful experiences helps you fulfill their potential. By seeing what goes into them, you can have them more often. However, you are more likely to have difficulty assimilating painful experiences. To facilitate that, notice what was at play in you during them and what you could have done differently. This includes how you might have been more considerate of yourself and your own needs as well as how you might have been more effective in handling others or events. Release any feelings and take any actions necessary to be complete.

How can you avoid re-experiencing pain when assimilating painful experiences?

The best way to avoid pain is to not avoid pain. If you tense up and brace against pain, you amplify it; if you embrace it, it lessens, because it is allowed to move through you and dissipate.

Bracing is for outgoing action: when you are throwing a ball, for example, you tense your muscles prior to the release. In bracing against pain, you do not release; you leave the tension there. Tense muscles are brittle. They can more easily be injured than those that are flexible, and do not let energy move.

There is always more to learn. If you knew how to do everything, you probably would not bother to incarnate. Your essence is interested in growth. You learned every skill you have, if not in this life, then before it. If you are to have more skills, you must learn them.

It is also true that there are skills you already have on a soul level that you have not yet uncovered. As you awaken to your whole self, there is less need to relearn what you already know. You make fewer mistakes that are similar to ones you made before. Your strides of growth speed up. Instead of "baby" steps, you take larger ones. Baby steps are valuable, too; they are more tedious, but they can make your education more thorough. Ultimately, no experience is wasted.

Grow at the speed that is most comfortable for you. Be

conscious of the choices you make day by day. Make the best ones you can, but do not judge yourself for prior choices. Every choice can lead to growth. If the results of prior choices are painful, they can teach you much—primarily what not to do. Learning what not to do can be of great value in developing mastery, although it doesn't have to be done through direct experience, which might be called "growing through pain."

Here is an analogy to illustrate growing through pain: Suppose that you are driving a race car down a track and you are not very conscious. The track has special heavy shock-absorbing guard rails on both sides so you cannot hurt yourself too much. You bump into the right rail. That, of course, jolts you and momentarily gets your attention, but you overcompensate and bump into the left rail. After a while you condition yourself to not move the steering wheel too much in either direction. You pretty much stay on course until the track turns a corner and you bump into the right rail again. You then condition yourself to turn the steering wheel a little to the left when you come to a corner. Painful as it is, bumping into the guard rails is useful; otherwise, you would go off the track. But if you were more conscious, you would see the track and choose to stay on it without needing to bump into the rails.

Although many people resist pain—they certainly do not want to bump into those rails any more than they have to— they often avoid joy as much or more. You might take an inventory of the ways you avoid joy, if you do. For example, if you look into someone's eyes, feeling blended and joyful, do you become embarrassed or uncomfortable with the intensity, making a joke or looking away? When you see something beautiful, such as a bouquet of flowers, do you just glance at it, or do you really look at it? A beautiful thing can withstand much looking, and the more you look, the more you can experience joy.

You tend to get what you focus on, and if you focus on

pain, even the avoidance of it, you tend to get it. Many people think that it would be irresponsible to focus on joy, that they would be like a child running amok. They would not pay their bills or go to work, if their work is not joyful (and it often is not). That is not actually the case. A child who runs amok may start off laughing but is likely to end up crying or screaming when he bumps into a guard rail. To sustain the experience of joy, there must be consciousness and mastery. It takes skill, balance, and wisdom to live a joyful life. To change analogies, it is like navigating a boat: If you know what you are doing, you can avoid the rocks and enjoy the beautiful day, moving with the constantly shifting winds. If you are a novice, you are more likely to hit a rock.

A key to growing through joy is making choices consciously, not merely intellectually, but with your whole being. That requires weighing everything relevant, not making a choice before you are ready, before you get a definitive confirmation from within that says, "This is right. This is the highest, most loving choice I can make here. It will result in the greatest amount of good for myself and others."

You make choices, large and small, continually. Everything you do, think, and feel is a choice. What you say and how you say it is a choice. How you walk and sit is a choice. Obviously, each choice does not call for deliberation, but you can increasingly bring consciousness into all you do by being aware while you do it.

You choose everything fundamental in your life. When choices are unconsciously governed by painful past experiences, pain and ineffectiveness result. The more conscious you are of your choices, the more effective and joyful you can be.

3 ❖ GROWTH WITH AWARENESS

You are not here on earth merely to grow, but you do grow. You grow whether you like it or not, whether you try to or not. You grow either unconsciously or with awareness. More commonly, people grow unconsciously: something happens, and they automatically react to it in some way; through what results, they learn something. Usually what results is unpleasant to some degree, so they learn what not to do. When you grow with awareness, you appraise situations without preconceptions, and consciously choose your response based on creative thought and the highest understanding available to you. The results of this are more likely to be pleasant, but as you respond consciously to whatever unpleasantness does arise, you transform it.

No growth occurs without making mistakes. In unconscious growth, people often repeat mistakes several times. When they finally learn the lessons of their mistakes, they generally learn them very well, but this is a painful and frustrating approach. When you make mistakes with awareness, you see them as gifts. You take full advantage of what they have to teach. You give thought to what led to them and how you could have handled things more effectively. You do not criticize yourself for making them. Rather, you might even congratulate yourself for taking risks, allowing you to come closer to your goal.

Most people sometimes grow unconsciously and sometimes with awareness, in varying proportions. Neither way is "wrong." Your essence is only concerned that you grow; in a sense, it does not care how you do it. If you vigorously resist all your lessons, that itself is a lesson—no experience is wasted. But as you gain expertise in this game we are all playing, you realize that it is more fun to grow with awareness, to make necessary mistakes but to avoid those that can be avoided.

GROWTH WITH AWARENESS

Souls who are new to the game learn mostly unconsciously. They do not yet have the skill to play the game consciously. Most people, though, continue growing unconsciously far longer than necessary. A goal of playing the game is to get better at it, which would include a movement away from unconscious growth toward growth with awareness.

Many people resist awareness. They would rather function unconsciously because they fear what they might become aware of, especially in themselves. However, true awareness is a loving, compassionate perspective. At first, there may be a need to see some ugly things, but one can view them as raw material for playing the game. If you started out knowing how to play the game perfectly and had nothing to learn, you would quickly become bored with it. All of us need challenges.

If a person looks in the mirror and sees a great deal of selfishness, for example, this fact of selfishness is neither good nor bad; it is simply a fact. He need not judge it, or on the other hand, make excuses for it. In looking more deeply into it, he might ask himself some questions: Is it all really selfishness?—maybe there are some other things mixed in with it. What are the reasons for it? How does it make him feel? What are its effects on others? And most important, what does he wish to do about it?

If he has been judging himself for being too selfish, he might say, "I am going to change. I am going to devote my life to others," but the reason for such a change would probably be fear. "I have been bad to be selfish," he might reason, "and if one is bad, one might be punished, so I am going to be good now." He goes to the opposite extreme and thinks only of others, perhaps running himself ragged and even ruining his health, or at least neglecting his own personal needs. Because he is motivated by fear and not by a love of expressing himself and sharing with others, after a while the pendulum would probably swing back. He might say, "I can't do this anymore; I'm going to go back to being selfish," at least to some degree.

If the person evaluating his selfishness comes to truly understand it, he can see how it has served him, what his "payoff" has been. He might then see that there are better ways of achieving the same thing. Perhaps he feels that he must look after himself because no one else is concerned about his well-being. If that is the case, he can consciously choose different, more satisfying means of having his needs met, such as developing mutually nurturing relationships. He might also make some choices about where he will draw the line in taking care of others, so he does not become overwhelmed. Although his former state of complete selfishness did not give him the experience that he was truly after, there are lessons in it for him to remember as he goes about creating a more balanced experience. As he becomes more concerned about others, he can also realize that he must live according to his own rules and choices.

If you are following other people's rules, you are like an artist to whom others dictate what to paint, with what colors, how big a canvas to use, and so on. We are not implying that you should do whatever you want to do without regard to others, and ignore their feedback. For one thing, you would be foolish not to take advantage of the information they offer, even when they criticize you or tell you what they think you should do. You can think about their points of view, and you may decide to incorporate some of them into your own. There may be something valuable in them even if you do not care for the way they offer them to you. But ultimately, you must decide what the highest way is for you. It is your game to play, and how you play it is your responsibility. Blaming others for it does not advance your game. In fact, it causes you to forget about it.

The game is the game of growth, expansion, and creativity. You use the challenges of life to win it. If you had an unhappy childhood, it is full of raw material for advancing your game.

Everyone can make the choice to live more consciously. If you fall back into living unconsciously, as you are likely to do from time to time, congratulate yourself when you notice it and then be more conscious. Do not be hard on yourself—falling back is part of learning the game.

You have free will, and have chosen the basic elements of your life, including your parents and the other key people with whom you play the game. You have also chosen where you live and what you do, and although it may be quite a challenge, you can change some of those choices. Perhaps you would like to move somewhere else, yet have little money. It might require some creativity but there is probably a way to do it. Many people work hard in their unconscious patterns but are lazy in playing the game when it comes to examining their preconceptions and taking conscious, creative action.

Sometimes spiritually-oriented people are passive in their lives. They think they should just accept whatever comes along without having any impact on it: "This happened, so it was supposed to happen." That is growing unconsciously. While it is wise to greet everything that comes along with loving acceptance, you cannot be in a situation without having an impact on it. Even leaving it has an impact. It is a matter of choosing what your impact is. Your creative task is to have the most constructive impact possible. Doing nothing may be the most helpful course, but taking useful action or leaving the situation might also be. Some people believe that if they make a choice, they are stuck with it. Therefore, they stay in situations when that is no longer constructive. You can change your choices.

Being conscious is a great gift. You may choose not to use it—that is your right. But the more you use it, the more you will want to.

4 ❋ THE SPEED OF GROWTH

Speed is relative. Let's say you are riding your bicycle and thinking you are going fast. Then, a car zooms by (and it is going slowly compared to its ultimate capacity) but an airplane overhead far surpasses its speed. Speed is not an absolute phenomenon. It can only be measured by comparing it to something else—for example, the speed of light.

Children are at a certain height one year and a greater height the next, yet do not usually notice the growth as it is occurring unless there are growing pains. A child's growth may seem slow compared to the growth of a cornstalk yet it has much significance for him.

There is no need to compare your growth to any particular standard. The human body must grow more slowly than a stalk of corn because it is a more complicated organism, for one thing. If your body were to grow one foot in a month, it would be quite painful and it would take years for the body to integrate that extra foot of height to the point where it could move gracefully.

Spiritual growth is sometimes stymied unnecessarily. If a cornstalk does not receive adequate water, sunshine, and fertilizer, it will not grow to its full height, at least not as quickly. Likewise, it is necessary to nurture growth in yourself. However, beyond a certain point, you cannot make growth occur faster.

Although relative speed may be appropriate, speed itself is not a virtue. Some people pride themselves on how quickly they get through something. Others take more time to do apparently the same thing, but who can say, in the long run, which way yields more benefit? All things considered, speed is just a matter of choice. There is no cosmic race. For one thing, there is no beginning and no end as you would think of it. We are all on a vast loop.

There are those who enjoy speed, such as race car drivers.

They go quickly and they enjoy the ride. Some people drive slowly and enjoy the ride. Some people drive slowly and are bored. And some people drive quickly and are tense. Whatever speed you choose, we recommend that you enjoy the ride.

5 ❋ EVOLUTION THROUGH CREATIVE PLAY

We are all in the endless process of spiritual evolution. Evolution is generally thought of as being painstaking and difficult. That is one way of experiencing evolution. It may appear to be slow because of the magnitude of what is evolving. If a wheel as big as a planet were spinning 60 m.p.h., it would look much slower than an automobile wheel at that speed. It is better not to judge that your personal evolution is too slow or too fast. It is what it is. Why not have the experience you are having rather than fighting it?

It takes hundreds of hours to make a fine quilt, but someone who loves to quilt probably does not think of it as a slow process. She knows that is how long it takes to make a good quilt. You could make a usable cover from one piece of fabric that would keep you as warm as a quilt would, but it would not be a quilt. Quilts tell stories; they pass along history to future generations.

You are engaged in creating a beautiful quilt. Its pieces are your experiences. The design of the square that you are sewing now comes from the joys and lessons of this lifetime. The other squares come from your previous lifetimes. Some are plain; some are fancy. Some are colorful; some are not. Some pieces are smooth and soft, while others have a rougher texture. All contribute to the quilt. Each person's quilt is unique. Some quilts are highly sophisticated, while others are simple, but all are beautiful.

MEDITATION

Close your eyes and imagine the design and colors of your quilt. Imagine what it feels like. Luxuriate in it. Whatever it is, it is beautiful. Love it. If there is sorrow woven into it, appreciate how it has strengthened the fabric. If there is ugliness in it, thank it for its message of beauty. If there is blood on it, know that it will wash out. If it is stained by tears, know too that this will be cleansed and only the true colors will remain.

Would anyone like to share their quilt?

Mine had a lot of depth to it. The squares seemed three-dimensional and were in deep, dark colors. There were birds above it.

You saw the depth and richness of your experiences. The birds, in this instance, represent something higher that is watching over you.

I zeroed in on a section of about eight or nine squares, predominantly reds and oranges, thick and soft like velvet. Between them were strips of green and yellow, as if you were above trees looking down through them with a lot of sun. It felt warm and energized, not driven but confident.

You have been enjoying yourself on the physical plane. You have become aware of the beauty of the earth and her gifts, which are many. You have allowed yourself to eat of the fruit of the trees that this planet gives you.

I saw black and green stripes. At first, I didn't like the black stripes, so I tried to substitute white ones, but it didn't work. Then I had black, white and green stripes. It was huge, extending in every direction without end.

We think you were observing your square from this life. You are working on it so closely and intently that it dominates your view. If you were to stand away from it, it would seem smaller. The black stripes represent the unknown to you, which makes up about half your life right now. As they say, black is beautiful. Embrace the darkness. When you do not know what is going to happen, you might think of it as a wonderful surprise in store. Since you have black stripes, the unknown is permeating your entire existence. The green represents the healing occurring.

At first, I saw defined shapes in many colors: blue, red, orange, and yellow. Then they blended into mountains, hills, trees, and water. I next saw pieces on it that were burnt. The last thing I saw was a deep velvet burgundy.
What do you think it means?

I suppose that the first part is my energy. The second part is how I use it in my love for the earth. The burnt areas are my hurt. The burgundy is my inner world that is deep and makes everything else look bright.

The orange, red, and yellow are the colors of a flame, and the blue is the color of a flame's cool center. You want the fire of your aliveness to burn in your relationship with the earth. If you are burned a little, that is all right. The velvet burgundy suggests comfort.

I got a large orange-yellow ring in a square quilt. Outside it were purples and blues. Inside were green and earth tones, the fall colors. A bright, beautiful flame came out of the center.

Like the previous quilt, yours symbolizes physical aliveness. The ring represents that which has no beginning or end. The purples and blues portray the spiritual world encompassing the physical.

Mine had two kinds of basic cotton material. One was a small, red-flowered print against a white background. The other was plain red. In the center was a large cut-out sun. I couldn't see the whole thing. I also saw large, cut-out tulips with long stems.

You are focusing a lot on earthy creativity, represented by the red and white floral squares, yet you know that it exists in a larger context, symbolized by the sun. The tulips remind you of other, larger experiences you have had creating something beautiful. Even though the red flowers are modest by comparison, they will grow. In other words, your creativity will become more of what you want it to be.

Incidentally, there are many valid ways of interpreting anything. When we share our ideas, we do not wish for you to think that they are "it." They are merely our "it." They may not be the whole "it" or your "it."

The way you grow the most easily is to enjoy your life. This does not mean that you shirk responsibility. On the contrary, you grow by enjoying whatever you choose to do, including what you choose to take responsibility for. Of course, not all circumstances are enjoyable in themselves, yet you can creatively play with how you handle them, maintaining your sense of humor and not taking them too seriously, while genuinely caring about them.

Children develop the complex skill of eye-hand coordination partly by drawing pictures, by playing with their crayons and finger paints. In other words, they grow by playing. What would happen if you said to a two-year-old, "You need to develop eye-hand coordination. I'm going to put you on a strict program so you can learn it by the time you are three-and-a-half. If you do not, you are going to embarrass us all. Therefore, I want you to copy these exercises"? It would not be a lot of fun, and he would not likely develop eye-hand coordination as well. It would be a slow and painful process.

There is much thought given to abundance. Abundance relates to joy. There are people who have millions of dollars but who do not have an abundance consciousness; they are unaware of having enough. There are people who are surrounded by others who love them but who do not feel abundance because they do not acknowledge it. Abundance consciousness is the heartfelt knowledge of having plenty. It springs from a feeling of connection to the whole. You may not have figured out yet exactly how you are going to pay the bills, but if you have an abundance consciousness, you will probably find a way.

Why is it that many people do not acknowledge their abundance and therefore have joy? It is primarily a matter of what you focus on. Regarding your physical body, for instance, if all you think about is the parts that are afflicted in one way or another, you will not have much joy in your body. You are excluding awareness of the parts that are working well. It seems natural to focus on what is not right. It is true that the parts that have needs call out to you to take care of them. If a muscle is sore, it calls out to be massaged. If your finger has a burn, it calls out to be healed—you might put some aloe vera on it. Yet if you give all your attention to what is wrong, you do not experience what is right as well. The point is to maintain an awareness of the whole.

There is a problem orientation in most people. This is a great contributor to the tendency to grow through pain rather than joy. The pain is what is focused on. A state of no pain is considered nirvana. Disagreeable and inconvenient events occur on a more or less regular basis on the physical plane, but the way you look at them determines your experience of them.

We are not suggesting going to the other extreme and denying your pain, denying that your finger has a burn and needs attention, or that something is inconvenient when it is. We are suggesting a balance, giving "equal time" to other facts that are also true. For example, when you acknowledge that one of your fingers has a burn, you can also feel the others that do not. When you acknowledge that your boss is a "pain in the ass," you can also be aware of your coworkers who are supportive. If you get to a point at which you see your experiences with a certain amount of objectivity and give credit where it is due, you tend to become more calm and enjoy what is going well in your life.

Problems are there to be solved. We are not suggesting ignoring them, thinking, "After all, I have these other things. I should feel lucky." If problems are nagging you, you may not have addressed them adequately. However, if you initiate a plan for solving them and maintain a balanced view, you will be able to keep them from dominating you.

EXERCISE

To maintain an awareness of the things that are right in your life, make written lists of them for different areas, reviewing them once or twice a day.

Why do we tend to focus on the negative?

Everyone has experienced a lot of crisis, if not in this lifetime then in others. Crisis stimulates the survival instinct. Suppose you lived through a fire that destroyed your house and crops. Finding food to eat and a place to live would, of necessity, dominate your attention, at least at first. When the negative constitutes a large part of what is going on, focusing on it to some extent is necessary for survival. Even in crisis, one can maintain a calm and constructive approach, but the tendency is to panic, especially when one doesn't trust one's ability to meet the challenges. Panic makes it harder to let go of survival fears after they are no longer warranted. Focusing on survival can then become a habit, and anything negative can look like a threat to survival. Recognizing that your basic survival needs are being met, you can let go of the habit and start seeing your life in a more balanced way.

Animals are creatures of habit or instinct. They are hardwired to function within certain boundaries given particular kinds of situations. Many people operate in the same way. It is apparently easier to be a creature of habit than a creature of reason, making new choices. There is a fear of consciously making choices. This is why habits are so persistent and so much more powerful in people's lives than they need to be. There is a place for habits but it would be valuable to break the habit of having so many habits, and have the habit of appraising situations in a fresh manner as they arise. You certainly grow more quickly and easily if you do that.

A lot of attention on the negative can be counterproductive. There are certain matters that need your immediate and direct attention, such as your house burning down. Other things need your indirect attention, such a health condition stemming from not exercising adequately. Rather than emphasizing and trying to eliminate symptoms (negative), it is more effective to start finding joy in using your body (positive); as a by-product, it will become healthier. Focusing on the negative is not very useful in this case, whereas focusing on a positive can solve the problem.

There are other negatives you cannot do something about at all at the time. You can simply acknowledge them and commit to dealing with them if and when you can. Focusing on them is a waste of time or worse—it can give them undue power over you. It is important to know the difference between what you can change now, what you can change over time, and what you cannot change at all. A common habit is to give as much attention to the things that cannot be changed (especially the past) as to those that can, becoming inflamed over all of them.

If a person is addicted to being inflamed, his current problems seem to grow to fit his capacity for inflammation. He is generally as upset about his problems today as he was yesterday, last year, ten, or even thirty years ago. It almost does not matter what the problems are. He does not accurately see them but views them through an addict's haze.

He is not truly interested in resolving them. Problems give him a sense of identity, a reason to live, something to suffer for.

People go to war not to solve problems but to express their inflammation. If people are truly interested in solving problems, the problems are usually solved. Part of your reason for being here is to be creative in meeting the challenges of the physical plane; in other words, to solve problems. If you did not engage with problems, you would be unemployed, in a sense. Some people like to call them opportunities, but we do not mind calling them problems. As mentioned, mathematicians love to solve problems—they find it fun.

People are less likely to go to war, throw tantrums, or complain ceaselessly if they know constructive ways to vent their feelings, and creative and effective ways to deal with their problems. Those who are chronically inflamed can learn to act more appropriately, allowing their inflammation to heal. Education in principles such as these is very important, and the best education is from example. People need to see examples of true problem-solving. The more you find creative ways to solve problems, the more you will inspire others to do the same.

What can you do to help someone who dwells on the negative to see the positive side of things?

You might find nonchalant ways of changing the subject to things he is enthusiastic or positive about. Avoid seeming to correct him for being overly negative. No doubt the things he is saying have at least some validity. If you preach, you will irritate him, putting distance between you and him. The first priority is to practice these habits yourself. They are "infectious." If someone is open, he will notice that you are having a better time than he is, and in some way, he will probably get it.

Is the quilt ever completed?

When you finish this quilt, you will start a new one.

6 ❀ JOY

Each person is designed to be an embodiment of joy. If you are interested in knowing whether someone is enlightened, notice the extent to which she embodies joy.

Joy is characterized by delight in the experience of the present. Joy is not driven by external influences. That is the primary difference between joy and pleasure. Pleasure is largely stimulated from without, whereas joy arises from within. There is nothing wrong with pleasure but pleasure cannot be relied upon because external influences are not always pleasurable. On the other hand, joy is reliable.

There are many varieties of joy. Not all are effulgent—some are low-key. One who has mastered joy has access to it in all circumstances, although the kind of joy you might experience walking through a garden on a spring morning is not the same as what you might when outer influences are painful.

Let's say that a loved one dies. You certainly feel your loss, and would prefer to have him remain with you in the flesh. However, joy can coexist with grief or any other emotion. The bond you had while he was alive changes, but you are still connected. You might, for instance, feel his elation in being released from his body. There can be extraordinary intimacy shared when someone passes over that is profoundly meaningful and exquisite.

If you have mastered joy, you see beyond external factors. You can have joy because joy arises from within.

How could joy be experienced if someone attacked you? On the personality level, this is a horrendous experience, but if you are repaying karma, you can feel the karmic ribbon burning away, and that could be joyful, even ecstatic. Again, joy can coexist with pain.

If you are mastering joy, you might see being attacked as a challenge, using the situation's stress to help you come fully into the present moment and transcend what is occurring, connecting with higher energies. You might seek to pour great love into and through your body to the other person. This can have a remarkable impact on those around you, particularly the one harming you. Most victims have not mastered joy and simply play out the mirror image of the victimizer. If someone has an experience of higher energy in the stress of that circumstance, he demonstrates the freedom of the realized soul. Jesus is an example of someone who mastered joy and had a transcendent experience when his body was harmed. He did not seek harm, but he handled it with mastery when it occurred.

There have been saints who sought to reach ecstasy through agony, and there are people who deliberately mutilate themselves in order to reach a higher experience. That is growing through pain. You need not go out of your way to find stress—ordinary life on the physical plane provides enough. It is true that the stress of pain can help you open and come into the present moment, but you need not go through physical harm, let alone self-mutilation, to come into the present moment. You can choose to be in the present because you love to be. But if pain is thrust upon you, you might as well use it for growth and turn it into a blessing.

In mastering joy, you do not deny pain. In fact, there can be no true joy if there is denial of pain or whatever is going on, because denial takes you out of the present moment. Denial numbs your experience. Joy heightens your experience.

Ill health is probably the most difficult challenge for the majority of people. When a stress is condensed into a short period of time, you can more easily marshal your fortitude than when it goes on and on, as with a chronic illness. There are those, nonetheless, who have a transcendent experience in illness, even when facing death and in much pain.

Although you do not need intense stress in order to experience higher energies, if you are busy in your day-today life and focused on externals, you may not get around to connecting all that deeply with your inner world. The forced inactivity that illness sometimes brings can give you the time, and the pain can give you the motivation, to contemplate and open to higher energies, as well as develop greater compassion and understanding. Letting go of fear about the outcome and focusing on bringing forth the energy of healing is the key. The pain may be transmuted or even eliminated. For example, endorphins, the body's natural painkillers, may be triggered. Whether or not the body heals, the bringing forth of higher energies is a blessing and inspiration.

I had an opportunity in the last couple of years to create my worst fear, which wasn't as dramatic as these examples: financial ruin. It was accompanied by a spiritual crisis, wondering how this could happen. As I was working through some of it, it occurred to me that there's a freedom in coming face to face with your worst fear. I'm now feeling that there isn't anything to really be afraid of anymore because I already got that over with, and there is joy in that. We don't know what resources we have to cope with those things until we actually do. I think that this probably applies to all the situations discussed.

Indeed. Fear is overblown for most people. If you encounter a rattlesnake, fear is an appropriate response. Fear is there to help you deal with danger, giving you extra adrenaline, but when it is chronic, it is harmful and unnecessary.

When someone has lived in the shadow of what is to him a tremendous threat, the experience of it is often anticlimactic. There is a realization that having invested so much energy into keeping this thing at bay, maybe it was not such a big deal. Certainly this realization of true perspective comes after the lifetime is completed if not during it. One reason that you often attract to you the experiences that you most fear is that having them is sometimes the only way that you will release the fear.

Most fear is fear of death. Financial fear has fear of death underneath it, because what happens if you do not have any money? If you cannot buy food or acquire shelter, you might get sick and die. Fear of punishment is certainly fear of harm, and the ultimate harm is death.

Sometimes fears are based on past experiences you were not equipped to handle. When there is too much intensity at once, you are not able to expand your capabilities fast enough; you snap instead of bend. For example, if you had a past life in which you were tortured, unless you had a very high level of mastery, it was undoubtedly very traumatic. Perhaps today, your fears mobilize at the slightest provocation to protect you from going through that again. Recognizing the source of your fears, and that the danger of being tortured is no longer present, can help dissipate them.

The ultimate goal in mastering joy is to reach a point where you cannot be traumatized because you can be joyful in any situation. That is a lofty goal, and though you may never meet it on the physical plane, it is worth working toward. In joyfully meeting challenges that stretch you but that are within your reach, you expand your capacity for joy. You do not master joy simply by being like a child who plays and has fun all the time in a stress-free environment. The ability to play and have fun is vital, but one's joy capacity is not very large if external influences can easily take it away. The many stresses of the physical plane give you the opportunity to develop it. Paradoxically, the greater your mastery of joy, the fewer unpleasant stresses you are likely to attract.

For some people, happy experiences are harder to handle than painful ones. These must be mastered as well. Those who had abusive childhoods, especially, may feel at their best when under strain and pressure, because that is what they are used to. Therefore, they are more likely to create painful experiences through which to grow.

Some people insist on having mostly painful growth because they are not willing to receive the necessary understanding any other way. You will probably have some painful experiences, but you can keep them to a minimum if you choose to grow through joy. You do not need to be excessively concerned about painful experiences because any of them, if utilized consciously, can be joyful for you. They may not be totally joyful, because of remaining areas of unconsciousness in you, but you can grow more conscious through working with them.

If joy is simply a function of being conscious, why does it have to be mastered?

Consciousness grows gradually and must be developed. Mastering joy involves learning how to be conscious and allow energy to flow freely in a variety of circumstances. This requires an adequate command of the necessary material as well as spiritual skills.

Suppose that you find it joyful to sing as you walk. You know how to handle that circumstance and be joyful in it. Then, all of a sudden, you are on the stage of the Metropolitan Opera House with five thousand people watching you, having had no rehearsal, and you do not know the music. You probably would not have a joyful experience because you do not have a command of that circumstance, and you have not yet learned to embody joy when singing for a very large group. That is something that would need to be practiced over time, starting with smaller groups.

Singers who obtain success too fast, who are not practiced enough in handling the energy of singing for a large group, may not have a joyful experience. Obviously, our example is outlandish—one would not suddenly materialize on the stage of the Metropolitan Opera. But no doubt there are experiences into which you could be thrust that you would not be capable of handling with joy. If you are wise, you simply turn down those opportunities, if possible, until you are ready for them.

During your first lifetime, you are totally raw; you have no mastery of joy. You may experience joy because of your connection to the Tao, like an infant to her mother, but when you are in a situation that is beyond your ability to handle—and at this point, there are many that are—your joy is likely to evaporate. You may panic, like an infant frightened by something unfamiliar. That is why you usually seek simple, safe environments, such as in a tribe, during your earliest lifetimes. Your spirit guides, who are more experienced, help you set up lifetimes that are appropriate for your level of skill. In time, you learn and gain confidence. Situations that formerly caused panic in you begin to be joyful.

Everything you go through is at least a little bit new. We are not suggesting that when you master joy, you act on the basis of precedent. The opposite is true: when you master joy, you are freed from precedent. You do not have to do things the same way you did them before. You can perceive and understand situations as they are, and be creative and appropriate in addressing them. You do not go into panic or automatic pilot, or shut down, closing your eyes and hoping for the best. You consciously make choices rather than reacting to external influences.

One who has fully mastered joy has mastered the physical plane. No one masters every aspect of the physical plane, but if you have had an adequate number of lifetimes in diverse settings, you have what might be called a well-rounded education, and you feel that you can handle the basics. We are not speaking of material skills, such as mastering the fingerings of a musical instrument; material skills generally have to be learned in each lifetime, although if you have learned them before, it goes faster. We are speaking of spiritual skills—for example, the development of a high level of musicality.

It is actually possible to be more joyful than children. For most people, children are the epitome of joy. There are not too many joyful adults around to indicate otherwise. But children have relatively limited capabilities. As an adult your capacity for joy is much greater.

MEDITATION

Take a moment to quietly be in the present. Feel joy coming forth from within. If you are ready to make the choice to grow through joy, whether outer experiences are pleasurable or painful, reach out to joy. Know that joy is always a possibility. If you have been carrying stress in your body, feel it release now. There is no longer a need for it. Joy to the world!

Part II

ESSENCE AND GUIDES

7 ❋ ESSENCE

WHAT IS YOUR ESSENCE?

Your essence is your higher self. It is spawned by the Tao into the dimensional universe, which consists of seven planes of existence. The core of it is the spark of the Tao that spawned it.

Just as your essence is an expansion of the Tao, your personality is an expansion of your essence. Before your essence begins incarnating, it is, you might say, a seedpod full of potential. It has had no experience, so it seeks all experience. It casts forth one seed, a piece of itself, into its first lifetime, and hence the game begins. Every experience on the physical plane expands your essence. If your essence had nothing to learn, it would not bother to confine itself within human bodies. The very limiting of an aspect of itself in a human body gives rise to more possibilities, more experiences.

Is it accurate then to refer to our wholeness, if the essence is always learning and expanding?

This is an apparent paradox, but you are always whole and complete even though you are continually growing. Your physical body is a symbol of this. It was complete—that is, having all its parts—when you were born, but it grew and matured for many years. In fact, it never stops changing.

All your parts make a perfect and complete whole. Knowing wholeness is integrating them, including them in your awareness. You can do this and still not know everything that there is to know in infinity. The possibilities of existence will never be exhausted. Your possibilities as an essence will never be exhausted. There is always more. Yet you are a whole being, consisting of all your parts. The greater your awareness of them, the more effective you are.

ESSENCE BOREDOM

Essence becomes bored when there is little growth occurring. If there is little growth occurring, it is because there is something stuck. Sometimes essence will generate a traumatic event to jar the personality loose because that is the only way to get through.

Your essence is neutral about how you grow, but growing through joy obviously feels better than growing through pain. It is only because people insist on growing through pain that this is the predominant way of growing at this time on earth.

Ultimately, there is no stopping growth. To make an analogy, if a four-year-old decides that he no longer wants to grow physically, he can wear very tight clothing and never take it off. After a while, his body will start ripping it and bursting buttons, and he will find it difficult to move, but he will still grow.

INTEGRATING WITH YOUR ESSENCE

As you stay in contact with universal knowledge through your essence, you increasingly find your right place in relationship to others. The machinery of your life moves more and more efficiently, and there is a flow that fills you with a sense of heightened well-being.

In this process, your essence receives pure, complex thought forms from the larger whole and distills them, giving your personality what is important for you to consciously know. Such cooperation draws to your essence greater knowledge because you are using it and therefore drawing it in. It also fosters a greater reciprocity between your personality and your essence. More and more, you become aware of being not merely your outer personality, but your whole being, your essence expressing through your personality. This allows you to integrate your personality so that it ceases to exist as if it were a separate entity. As long as you have a physical body, you have some sense of separation, but it is reduced. This brings healing.

A technique for fostering such integration is to think of the words "I am" as meaning your whole being, including your essence. Then, when you say "I," you are consciously speaking from the whole of you, helping you come into alignment and identification with your wholeness.

Your wholeness is part of the universal whole. As you grow, more and more aspects of the whole, both internal and external, are blended into what you think of as "I." That includes other people. Complete conscious unification with the universal whole will probably not occur for you on the physical plane, but you can deliberately add more and more into your identity through connecting and identifying with other people and your environment, seeing them as part of you. That is a greater challenge with those who seem contrary to you, and it is quite significant to your growth when you accomplish it.

Essence and personality are two aspects of you. Neither should dominate. If you are "blissed out" on your essence to the point where you are not experiencing your personality anymore, you may as well go back to the astral plane. But if you are experiencing only your personality, you have forgotten what the game is about. Your conscious awareness, if properly placed, is not fully at the level of personality, yet not fully at the level of essence. It partakes of both.

ESSENCE CONTACT

Essence contact is a direct, clear, and powerful connection with essence. It occurs either internally, between an individual's essence and personality, or externally, between the essences of two people whose personalities are adequately open. It results primarily from genuine desire. The reason that stress often brings about essence contact is that under stress, there might be the desire—if you are hanging from a cliff, grasping crumbling rock, you might start praying. Because of the severity of that situation, an opening may occur in you that would not otherwise. But your essence does not require that you be under duress in order to make contact. The best way to develop essence contact is gradually, a little bit at a time. We recommend that you keep opening to your essence on a daily basis. Ask for its input and energy. Gradually, you start to have your essence properly represented in your life, if it is not already, just as the healing of your emotions allows your emotional self to be represented in your life. Every part of you deserves to be integrated into your life.

THE BIG PICTURE

Your essence decides the big picture, and your personality, the details. Your essence sets the course and your personality carries it out. Essence is more adept than personality at projecting the probable outcome of certain actions, and will block and reign them in if they are significantly off track. However, essence is not all-knowing. Fundamentally, it incarnates for the enjoyment of creating and adventuring into the unknown. This really is a game, in a sense the only game there is.

INITIATIVE

Do not assume that your essence or spirit guides have better specific ideas than you do on a personality level. Your essence delights in your coming up with ideas that complement its general vision.

IDENTITY

We are told to identify with our higher self. Although I feel a connection with my higher self, I don't identify with it. I sometimes get guidance from it that doesn't make sense to me. Can we just "be" our higher selves?

You could describe the self as being made up of the conscious, subconscious, and superconscious selves. Each of these three levels of self in turn has many facets. You can identify with the whole of yourself, including all its parts. Your superconscious is your higher self, or essence. It is the part of you with the overview. It is wise to strongly consider the overview, but your subconscious gives you much important information, too. Your conscious self is your decision-making and control center where your three levels of self can come together and co-create.

When your conscious self is isolated and dictatorial, it is the "false personality" or ego. When it is fully connected with both your subconscious and your essence, there is a fluid interchange that allows all your parts to integrate so you become a whole person. This is the "true personality."

When you are making a decision in true personality, you gather information and experience internal feedback to it, developing an inner consensus so that it becomes clear what your best choice is. All your parts are represented in the process.

When you say "I am," it does not represent only your higher self. All your parts are essential, or they would not exist. The higher self is "higher" only in the sense of having an overview, not of being better.

Your personality is valid. The goal is not to eliminate it, but to integrate it with your essence. The more you integrate it, the more you grow.

All growth is a result of essence contact. Contact with your own essence leads to growth, expanding your experience of self. When you also contact the essence of another person, there can be much further expansion.

All personalities start out in separateness. When the infant is delivered out of the womb and the essence incarnates, the personality is not yet very developed, so essence can be sensed. But you could not say at that point that the personality is integrated into the essence, because there is not much personality to begin with. Infants cry when they need to be fed or have other physical needs met. This is obviously not indication of complete identification with essence. Still, infants are recognized as being beautiful as they are.

The most evident aspects of a young child's behavior spring from the specific nature of her physical body; for example, some bodies are naturally more passive while others are more active. As she gets older, her personality becomes stronger. The more it develops, the more independent or separate she becomes, both from her parents and from her essence. It is necessary for her personality to develop if she is to integrate with her essence—otherwise, what is there to integrate? Someone with an inadequate sense of self cannot manifest his essence. Although it seems paradoxical, you must find separateness before you can find oneness. Separateness here refers to individuality, uniqueness, or differentiation, not to arbitrary isolation. Even when you are focused on developing your uniqueness, you can feel connected to the whole.

Integration with your essence is an essential part of the spiritual path.

LIKE PARENTS AND CHILD

Is it accurate to describe the relationship between the essence and personality as a teacher/student relationship?

It is closer to parents and child. The reason your essence sends your personality into the world is so your essence can learn from the world, not so your personality can learn from your essence. If your essence already knew the things that it wanted your personality to learn, it would not bother incarnating. Your essence might know principles, but needs to incarnate to "flesh out" its knowledge.

Your essence is rather like a couple who has many

ESSENCE

children so that the children can help out with the family business. In that analogy, your personality is one of the children of your essence; your reincarnational (past-life) selves are the others. The family business is what your essence wants to accomplish throughout all its lifetimes on earth.

Good parents try to help their children avoid unnecessary pitfalls but know that they cannot have their experiences for them or limit what they need to experience in order to learn. They give the right amount of freedom. Just so with your essence.

Although there is a trend toward parents teaching their own children, usually parents send their children to school so that other people can give their children input. Varying points of view stimulate growth in the child. If the only adults with whom children come in contact in their education are their parents, they do not get a balanced education. In this analogy, your personality's teachers include all your experiences and every important person in your life, as well as your guides and other friends on higher planes.

Your essence should be respected, just as you might respect your parents, listening to what they have to say but making your own decisions, taking all factors into account. You are fully responsible for what you do no matter what your parents say.

Suppose that you have wise and loving parents whom you respect, but you also have a beautiful mate, children, and siblings whom you also love and cherish, and your decisions affect all of them. If as a son or daughter you were to automatically obey your parents and disregard what your mate, children, and siblings feel, you would not truly be an adult. Being excessively tied to your parents keeps you childish. Your task is to take each family member's needs and views into account and come up with solutions that work for everyone. You may value and weigh your parents' views more heavily than any other individual view because they have had more experience than anyone else. Nevertheless, their position is not yours. They are not standing in your shoes and they do not have to live with the choices you make. They are not all-knowing. As their child, you build on their experience and move in new directions. Repeating their lives is not your purpose. After due consideration, you must make the decisions that feel best to you. If later you find that they were right, you can grant them that, yet you have to know for yourself. It is not so terrible to make a mistake. Mistakes help you learn.

You do a much better job when making decisions that affect all your family members if you are connected and communicating with them. Likewise, you are constantly making choices with your conscious mind that affect you on many levels. Connecting and communicating with the various aspects of yourself allow you to know what is actually happening so that you can make the best possible choices.

The analogy of parents and child for the essence and personality is limited. The relationship is actually much more intimate than that because your essence is the core of who you are.

THE COMING FORTH OF YOUR ESSENCE

Each essence is unique. No matter how highly developed it is, it continues to advance. At the same time, it is perfect as it is.

The more highly developed your essence, the more pressure it brings to bear in your personality. What you call enlightenment occurs when the force of your essence against the constraints of your personality grows to the point that your essence comes forth and manifests. This coming forth is quite dramatic with some people; with others, it is gradual; and with many, of course, it does not happen at all.

When a highly developed essence manifests, there is

more to manifest than with one of lesser attainment. However, every essence is beautiful and wise in its own way. There is simple wisdom, and there is more advanced wisdom based on greater experience. Once your essence manifests, there is still much to be learned but the learning tends to be more through joy than through pain.

THE TECHNICOLOR SELF

You look quite different to us when we look at you energetically instead of through a channel's eyes. Energetically, you appear rather like the samples of watercolor paints that a creative paint manufacturer might employ to foster sales of his beautiful pastels and rich, bright shades. You have never seen some of them before. When you are in harmony with your essence, your aura is a full technicolor revelation of you. Those who are less alive look more dull, like the sepia Kansas in *The Wizard of Oz*; there is not a lot of color or magic in their lives. As you progress on the spiritual path, your innate color fills in.

Imagine a cartoonist sketching a duck in pencil, and then painting canary yellow on his web feet, the white on his bottom, blue in the background, and so forth, until the color completely fills in. This is a little bit like what it can be for us to watch you over the years. Black and white cartoons can be entertaining and do the basic job, but full-color cartoons have another dimension.

So here you are, going over the rainbow into the land of Oz to meet the wonderful wizard that is you. He is sometimes popularly known as your higher self or essence. In this case, the wizard *is* a wizard. You might fear that you are going to find out that he is just a bumbling middle-aged gentleman pulling down the handles and making a lot of noise and sparks. If so, this is one story that could be rewritten in your mind. Instead, you could see yourself receiving a warm welcome from a truly wonderful wizard who is also a friend of the witches of all four directions. It is not as dramatic as seeking broomsticks, but you have done that script and are now ready to experience the power of your own selfhood. You do not have to fight witches to do that.

8 ❊ WORKING WITH SPIRIT GUIDES

Each person is the leader of a team assembled to achieve tasks. You organize your team prior to each lifetime. Some of your teammates are also currently inhabiting human life forms—other people. The rest are not. These discarnate essences are sometimes referred to as spirit guides or helpers. Everyone has at least one guide. Those with larger life tasks often have several. Most guides work with more than one person, but your primary guide focuses on you.

There is much misunderstanding about spirit guides. A spirit guide is like a personal trainer. If you decide to hire a personal trainer to help you work out, you do so partly because of the objectivity that she can bring. You may know as much or almost as much about proper exercise technique, but you cannot see yourself. Of course, the exercise facility may be mirrored, and there are times when looking in the mirror is useful—this is why they are on the walls. But if you spend all your time looking in the mirror, you will not be effective in working out. Your trainer may also hand you the equipment you need, and when you do not feel like doing another set, he may remind you of the task you chose. Spirit guides perform similar functions.

When you were between lives, you may have been a spirit guide for others, including those who are guiding you now. Those who are fairly new at being a spirit guide undertake an apprenticeship. One does not become a primary spirit guide before one is ready. Guides are learning as much through their partnering of you as you are.

Spirit guides are not perfect, and some guides do better work than others. Some are more experienced than others. You generally get the caliber of guidance you need and can handle. Those on the spiritual path often have exceptionally good guidance because they can make use of it.

Your guides are usually in roughly the same point in their

development as you are, although being nonphysical, they are not subject to the illusions of physical existence, giving them greater clarity and objectivity. When you were in elementary school and had just learned how to divide, you may have been better at teaching it to your classmates than your teacher, who probably had long before forgotten what he went through to learn division. For the same reason, it is useful to have guides who are not too far ahead of you.

It is the natural design of things to help one another along the way. As the poet said, no one is an island. Some people are prone to say, "No, don't help me. I'd rather do it myself." That is all right—there are times when you seek to meet a challenge alone, but you do not have to do it all alone. Coming to the physical plane is too rigorous to attempt without assistance. In fact, you never do it all alone. There is really no such thing as doing it all alone, although you can refuse to receive the help you are offered.

Most people are not consciously aware that they have spirit guides, but may occasionally "hear a voice" such as one telling someone not to board an airplane that later crashes. Many of those who board the plane may be ignoring such warnings. A competent spirit guide checks out planes before you get on them and will, in general, be aware of the condition of your automobile and your condition in terms of driving it. Job number one for your primary spirit guide is to help you stick around so that you can accomplish your life tasks. Some people make this job very challenging for their guides. It is not your guides' responsibility to keep you alive; they merely support you in your choice to accomplish certain tasks, which you will not do if you die prematurely.

Spirit guides live in astral substance (just as you live in physical substance), so that is the primary medium through which they work with you. It requires an enormous amount of effort for them to slow down their vibration enough to do things like manifest physical apparitions, so instead, they usually manipulate energy through astral substance.

Imagine a game at a party in which you put on a blindfold and you are seeking to move from point A to point B. Your teammate has the job of letting you know whether you are getting warmer or colder in approaching point B, so as you walk off course toward a wall, he says, "No, no, no!" You turn and go off toward another wall. "No, no, no, no, no!" he says again. Finally, you get warmer. "Yes, yes, yes!" he encourages, so you keep moving in that direction. If then you are about to walk into a table, he needs to coach you around it.

Guides generally do not yell in your ear, but they do let you know whether you are getting warmer or colder. If you are about to do something that is not in accordance with your life task and that would set you back, your guide may pull energy away from that direction. If it is really serious, he might gather together a large group to pull energy away from that direction. How might that feel to you on the physical plane?

Suppose that you are offered a job that, unbeknownst to you, is going to lead you in some directions that are not appropriate for you. The job looks very good to you on paper, including an excellent salary. Perhaps because of blind spots in you, or just information that is not available for you to know, you do not see that the main people you would be working with would be very draining on your energy at a time when you are seeking to do other things. So you are moving merrily along toward accepting this job and then you feel the energy being drawn away from it. You may feel it emotionally: all of a sudden, something does not seem right. You may find that the process of being hired there bogs down because people get busy with other things. They are feeling the energy being pulled away as well. Your guides might enlist the help of the guides of the person doing the hiring, informing them that this is negative for you or for all concerned, if that is the case. Those guides may trigger in him a negative reaction or aversion to you.

You may have a tire on your car that is old and has weak places on it. Left on its own, it might have lasted another week, but when you go out in the morning to drive off to your second interview, you find that it is flat. The guide would not have stuck a pin in it, but may have been able to energetically manipulate it to accelerate its movement toward its natural end of being flat. On the other hand, if your guides see that there is a weak tire and you need to get somewhere, they may send it energy rather than withdraw energy from it so that it can last until you get it changed, if possible.

We do not want you to think that every flat tire is the work of your guides and that every job that you do not get is sabotaged by them. Like a good coach or trainer, they intervene only when it is necessary. Most of the time, they just watch you "do your thing." If it does not matter whether or not you get a certain job, they will likely do nothing. Let's say that there are three possible jobs and they all look equal from the standpoint of your life plan. If it seems likely that you will get one of them, they may not do anything. You might look at these three jobs and say, "Job number one is, from my vantage point, the best one because it provides day care on the facilities and a better vacation schedule." Your guides may know nothing about those factors or may not be concerned about them because it does not affect your larger life plan. However, if you ask them to help you get this job, they will probably cooperate with you. That is what they are there for, and they like to have opportunities to develop their skills. If you are religiously inclined and pray to God, which we define as the overall consciousness of the universe, God will probably ask your spirit guides to give you a hand. Guides are part of what you might call God's crew supporting the physical plane. Your guides are in touch with their guides and teachers, who are in touch with theirs, and so on, all the way "up" to God. On higher planes, the guidance structure is different, but there is always support available.

Guides or teachers on any plane should not be seen as superior; they are colleagues. If you constantly say to them, "Do what you think is best," you are not participating in your process as fully as you might. Of course, it is sensible to be humble and acknowledge that there are times when you do not see what is needed. If you ask for something and it works out differently, there may be good reasons for this; it is good to be flexible. But you are the captain of your ship, and your leadership is needed. Do not become dependent on your guides. Do not look for them to lead the way. Occasionally, it is appropriate for your guides to take initiative and make suggestions—it is a team, after all; you are working together—but you are the head of your team.

It is true that guides see many things you cannot. On the other hand, you can see things your guides cannot see because you are here on the physical plane. Suppose that you are making a purchase and you would like some advice on it. Your guides can help you discern certain types of factors. However, they do not see color in the same way you do, for example. They can see, you might say, the vibrational or astral aspect of the color, and how it might affect you energetically; that is all they are qualified to read. You need to use your own discretion to determine whether the color will "go" where you are putting it. You might channel them so that they can look out at your prospective purchase through your eyes, and they can think back to when they were physical. Then they might say, "We like this other color better." For this to occur, though, you must be adept at channeling them and they must be adept at being channeled. Generally, guides do not often work with you in this manner. Besides, it is more important which color you like better.

Guides are different from higher-plane teachers. We are teachers from the causal plane. We have many more students than a guide would have "guidees." There are over a thousand of us in the Michael entity, and collectively we have over 100,000 students, some physical, some astral, and a few on the lower causal plane. That is a fairly high teacher/student ratio. If you are our student, we cannot be constantly looking over your shoulder, nor would that be helpful insofar as what our function is in your life. If spirit guides are like personal trainers, we are like special consultants. We deal with a larger picture still. When you come to us with questions, we often consult with your guides, although we remember our own work as guides and can do some of the things guides do. Due to our position relative to you, there are certain things with which we can be very helpful, and others with which we have less to offer. We do not seek to replace your relationship with your guides. We are not an "all-purpose entity"! If we were all you needed in terms of guidance and teaching, we would be the only ones around.

We are not the biggest "cheeses." The highest source available is the infinite soul. However, the infinite soul is very potent and is also rather unnecessary most of the time. The infinite soul is an embodiment of the Tao that expresses through one of the three high planes: the messianic—Jesus manifested the infinite soul from the messianic plane; the buddhaic—Buddha obviously manifested from this energy; and the mental—Lao Tsu and Krishna manifested from the mental plane [see glossary]. Teachers from these three high planes are more concerned with the larger spiritual dimensions of life, whereas your guides and causal plane teachers are more concerned with the functional side of life. Both are essential. Higher here means broader, not better. In a corporation, there are those at the top who chart the generalized course of the corporation, and there are others in the field who decide how the specific needs will be handled. You could not successfully have one without the other.

Beyond the high planes is the Tao itself and, in fact, all this is included in the Tao. The Tao is the All That Is, but the term mainly refers to what is not in manifestation. The Tao is the source. It made up this seven-plane game in the first place, which is why there are teams. You could say that the Tao is the stadium in which you play the game. Ultimately, not only is everyone in the universe playing the same game, but everyone is on the same side. Although there are teams, the game is not competitive.

If you begin to feel alone, remember that you are the captain of a terrific team. Ultimately, you cannot lose. However, you can have more or less fun playing the game. The question, "Are we having fun yet?" is a good one.

We are not belittling the challenges that arise in life; they are part of the game, after all. But because they are usually not seen from a larger perspective, they are often taken more seriously than is helpful.

Learn to use your guides. Ask not only for their help but for greater insight. Ask for better tools for handling the challenges that arise. The tools will come to you, one way or another. Some people report going to a bookstore and being hit on the head by a book falling off the shelf. Your guides do have a sense of humor! Such experiences help make it obvious that you are guided and assisted.

Your game—your life task—is what you signed up for. Some people are a little hasty in planning their lives but you probably had good help with yours and did not take on more than you can handle. Sometimes things take an unexpected turn and it is wise to retreat. In general, however, unless you have gone out of your way to make negative karma for yourself, your life is about right for you in terms of your capabilities. If it seems too hard, maybe you are trying to do it all alone. There's nothing wrong with asking for help if you are sincerely doing all you can. The support of others does not replace your own efforts; it supplements them. It is not "do it for me" but "do it with me."

Some people cannot accept help from others, even from their guides, because of low self-esteem. They think they do not deserve it. They think they if they receive help, they are taking help away from others: "No, I'll struggle along all by myself here. You go help someone else who really needs it. I'm all right," they may say, as they collapse on the ground! Can you imagine what team sports would be like if everyone took this attitude? "No, I will get the football over all by myself. Yes, I know that twelve people are about to tackle me, but that is all right. I will try to do it myself." The game of life is a team sport.

Mostly, we have emphasized the individual's game. There are collective games as well. Everyone on earth is part of a collective game agreed upon by all. There are also games played by smaller groups of people. Your game is part of these larger games. If you think that you cannot play the larger game because you are too busy with your own, you do not understand the game. When you truly play your own game, you are playing the larger game. You cannot help it. What is appropriate for you is appropriate for the whole. Perhaps you are unclear about what is appropriate for you, but some part of you knows. If you ask, your guides will help you see it.

Your guides are usually old friends. They are not there to make your decisions for you. They will tell you what they think, sometimes loudly, sometimes not. Accept their advice graciously. Often they know things you cannot know, but do not assume that they are always right. They are not, and if you automatically follow the advice of others, you will not develop your choice-making skills. Work with them and with everyone else on your team. Play your part on the teams of others in whatever ways feel right for you. We are all both teachers and students to one another because we are all ultimately one. There is great similarity between life lessons from person to person, yet every situation is unique. This provides the perfect opportunity to hone your skills in playing the game of life.

Do guides ever go too far and form karma?

WORKING WITH SPIRIT GUIDES

Guides do not form karma in the sense of a compelling debt that must be repaid. They do go too far from time to time, just as you do; that is a part of learning. However, generally they are well trained and supervised, their intentions are benign, and their methods are gentle, so it is unlikely that they would do much harm. However, if they do make a serious mistake at your cost, they will probably want to make it up to you one way or another, in the spirit of reciprocity, just as a friend might. They may agree to let you do some experimental guiding of them, for example. They may also undertake more training.

How can you learn to communicate well with your spirit guides?

A good way to communicate with your spirit guides is through meditation. If you allow yourself to be in a highly relaxed state and allow your imaginative faculty to be free, you can simply imagine your spirit guides. For example, you might ask to communicate with your primary spirit guide. After you have asked, just start imagining what he looks like. His appearance can be anything because those on higher planes do not have physical form. They appear to you in whatever form is comfortable for you. Even if you think that you are just making up an image, you are probably not. Accept whatever form comes to you, whether it is a stately Indian prince or a shaggy puppy dog, and start having a conversation with it in your imagination. Ask questions and listen for answers. If you do not get answers, make them up. After a while, something will begin to flow. You can have quite specific conversations with your guides, but it is easier to begin with more general questions. It is a good idea to have a tape recorder or a pad of paper handy to record your answers so you can review them later.

This is just one technique for getting in touch with your spirit guides; there are many others as well. Your guides always hear you, so you do not have to be concerned about that. You may not hear their answers back directly but they answer you in one way or another. Your primary challenge is to ask clearly and precisely.

Is there a maleness or femaleness to guides? Does a woman have a woman guide, and vice versa?

There is no actual gender when you are nonphysical. Almost everyone has had many lives both as male and female. Each soul, however, is to some degree more highly charged with either male or female energy. Usually, but not always—rules are made to be broken, as they say—if you are higher in male energy, you have a higher male energy primary guide, and vice versa. You alter this, though, for specific purposes. Also, if you are higher in male energy but in a female body, your guide may also be higher in male energy but appear to you in the female form that it took in a life when it knew you, if there was one. So, you might have a guide with a female name or in female dress as you imagine it, but it might be rather aggressive or more outwardly focused in its style with you.

If you and your primary guide both have higher male energy, you probably have at least one secondary guide who has higher female energy working closely with you to teach you about the balance.

Your primary guide helps you manage the overall pattern of your life. Your secondary guides help you with specialized tasks. If you are a musician, you may have a guide who works with you on music. If you are focusing on a spiritual path in your life, you may have one that works with you strictly on spiritual attainment. And so on. If you want a guide on a new subject, you can ask for one. There are plenty of unemployed spirit guides looking for work. As we mentioned earlier, they receive as much benefit from guiding you as you receive from being guided. However, if you are a difficult "client," you might have more difficulty finding one of the caliber that you want. Of course, there are lessons in that as well.

From what you are saying, I know that even when I was a little girl, my guides and teachers were around me. I just want to thank you all for what you provide. It is so useful for all of us down here.

Your guides appreciate your acknowledgment of their part in your life. You have probably found that when you do things for people who do not thank you or show any sort of gratitude, you are less inclined to want to work with them. The game itself is its own reward, but it is important to thank your guides and teachers, and all those in your life who enrich you. This opens you to receive more.

Could you comment on the usefulness of Tarot cards, Rune stones, things like this? Can spirit guides help you interpret them?

Yes. When you work with divination tools, your essence (in partnership with guides who specialize in that particular system) determines, if you are open, what cards, stones, or whatever, will come up. Then your own guides can help you to understand what their implications are. That is a good way to work with your guides.

Could spirit guides be channeled through someone without the channel being aware of it?

Yes. People are sometimes responsive to your guides if they care about you and want to meet your needs in the best possible way. Generally, information comes to them intuitively rather than through direct, word-for-word channeling.

Once in a while, a guide or another nonphysical being may look at you through the eyes of a child or pet. That could be called nonverbal channeling.

I have a schizophrenic teenage son who seems to be communicating with negative discarnate energies.

This is not unlike your son hanging out with members of a street gang rather than with those who support his growth. This is not "bad"; it is simply not very growthful. At some point, he will probably tire of that and seek to grow again. Then he will open again to his guides.

Guides are like therapists who are supervised for a number of hours when they begin their careers. They may not yet be very expert, but at least their intention is usually to help.

What can you do to focus better on what your guides are saying when they are all speaking at the same time?

You could simply ask them to speak one at a time.

How does the help you receive from your guides differ from that of your essence?

Generally, your guides focus on the external factors of your life, and your essence, the internal. Your guides help you open to your essence and complete your life tasks. Your essence, which is a part of who you are, thereby experiences expansion. Your essence encourages you to deal with and release inner blocks, and your guides help you set up your life to facilitate this.

MEDITATION

Imagine that all your guides are gathered around you. See

how beautiful they are, how much love they have for you, and how much fun they are. Enjoy being part of this team and the sense of connection it brings you.

Part III

SPIRITUALITY

9 ✺ THE LARGER VIEW

A FOUNTAINHEAD

You are a source unto yourself, a fountainhead of life. You connect into the whole in a unique manner, with your own webs of connections, both on the physical plane and to higher planes.

UNIVERSAL ENERGY

The physical plane is not separate from the higher planes. It is like the skin of the body of the universe, its outer edge. Where there is openness, energy can be poured out from within the body through the "skin."

REALITY

Life is far more complex and fluid than most would acknowledge. Human understanding is not possible without simplification, but those who wish to experience higher states of consciousness must destructure their thinking in order to accommodate more reality.

WORDS

Words are symbols of realities. Words are not realities except as words. Experience brings knowledge of what is behind words.

SEEKING

I have a feeling that what I am seeking is not on this plane. Could I have made a wrong choice, or is it that my time on the physical plane is done?

It is not that you are being guided to leave the physical plane, but that you are feeling an impulse to bring something higher into the physical plane, to connect with it inside yourself and help it to find form so that you can share it with others in ways that it can be received. It is true that what you are seeking is not of the physical plane, but you can access it from any plane. It is, fundamentally, your essence.

10 ❈ LIFE COURSE

DESTINY

Is it true that each of us has his own destiny in life, and if it is, then how do we learn what it is?

The concept of destiny is full of misconceptions. There is destiny in the sense that before you begin your life, you plan it, like an architect planning a building. However, even in construction, once work begins on a site, changes may need to be made, such as substitutions of materials and alteration of the floor plan, due to unforeseen circumstances or shifting needs. When this occurs, the basic character and function of the original design can still be honored, but it might look substantially different than the way it was envisioned.

In planning your life before incarnating, you know in general what you want to accomplish, and you usually make several alternative plans for achieving it. Since everyone has free will, you never know for certain who will do what, or when, so you want to be ready. Even so, you do much improvising, and your life may turn out to look very different than you anticipated. That is all right—it is part of the game.

Your destiny is the destiny you yourself chose, what you want to achieve in this life. It may or may not be specific in nature. You might have specifically wanted to be a writer, for example, or you may have simply wanted to communicate to others your understanding of how life works, which could be accomplished through writing, speaking, acting, singing, or dancing, and through different types of media, such as film, theatre, or television.

Usually, following your deepest longings will lead you to your life task. What you most love to do, what gives you the greatest sense of purpose, is likely to be along the lines of what you planned for this lifetime. If you have many apparently conflicting impulses, it may be because you have a number of tasks. You may choose to accomplish them one at a time, or you may find ways to fuse them and accomplish them together.

FREE WILL

The idea that there are no accidents implies predestination. How does that fit with free will, the idea that we have the right to choose?

It is true that many apparent accidents are karmic or preplanned, but in those cases, the people involved have still chosen them on some level, if not on the conscious level. The accidents were not imposed on the people involved by some outside "destiny."

There are also, actually, true accidents. For example, some car wrecks are simply due to carelessness, intoxication, or being "in the wrong place at the wrong time." You do make a basic plan for your life, but you do not follow it like an automaton, and mistakes do happen. There is some reason for everything that occurs, but it is not necessarily "cosmic" in nature, so it is wise not to generalize in this regard.

Having the right to choose does not imply that you choose everything that happens to you. Obviously, others make choices that affect you, and many circumstances are beyond your control. However, you can always choose your response.

THE VALUE OF ACKNOWLEDGMENT

Acknowledging the past and present allows you to build on them, so you can grow by making new mistakes rather than repeating old ones. An analogy is noticing what is in your wardrobe. It makes you aware of things to give away, making room in your closet for new clothes. It makes you aware of forgotten things that you might like to wear, as well as items needing repair or cleaning. Analyzing past purchases and knowing what you have helps you buy new things you will enjoy and can use. In other words, acknowledgment can make your choice-making more effective.

Acknowledgment also brings the power of your consciousness to bear on how things are, allowing them to change.

WHERE TO LIVE

If you sense that you are not where you would most like to be, you might, in meditation, ask for names or pictures of places where there are people with whom you have significant spiritual agreements, or where, in your life plan, you are interested in achieving certain goals. You may get one place or several. You can then visit them or learn more about them in other ways. See which one feels most right or seems to work best for you.

NAMES

I've been thinking about changing my last name legally in the next year, and I want something light and comfortable. I'm getting out of a marriage. I don't want his last name, and I don't want my maiden name.

A change of name, even through marriage, is stressful. Stress is not bad—all change creates stress, and through stress there can be growth. But, of course, you do not want to overdo it.

Since you are leaving a marriage, you are already dealing with a lot of stress. If you wish to minimize the stressful adjustment of a name change, you might explore names that are in one way or another similar, either in rhythm, rhyme, or ethnic derivation, to your married or maiden names.

You might also think of people you greatly admire, either in history or literature, for ideas. A name that is highly symbolic can give you both a standard to live up to and, by the same token, additional stress, so such a change should not be undertaken lightly. Names have much power on the physical plane. This is not said to discourage you, but to give you some things to think about.

11 ❊ NEW AGE MODALITIES

RIGHT FOR YOU

What do you think of the _____ workshop? Is it recommended to use this type of philosophy?

You can perhaps understand that it is not appropriate for us to say "yea" or "nay" to any particular path. For one thing, it may be useful for one person and not for another, so the question is whether it is for you. If you look into it enough, you will likely have a gut feeling about it. If you have any hesitation, then it probably is not right for you. If you do not know yet, you have not looked into it enough.

If you have not yet developed your own facility to perceive what is in alignment with your purposes, and you rely on the recommendations of others, you will likely do what is right for them rather than for you. Even worse, you may do what they think is right for them, and is not, and is even less appropriate for you.

There is merit in this program, as there is in most programs.

People should be where they feel they belong. If the New Age movement does not feel like home to someone, she should not be involved with it.

MEDITATION

There is no right or wrong experience in meditation. People who meditate regularly are sometimes bothered by the fact that some of their meditations feel high, and some feel like nothing much happens, or so-called negative things come up. What comes up is generally what needs to come up. It is your next step.

OUT-OF-BODY EXPERIENCES

Do you recommend out-of-body travel?
It depends on the individual. Some people first need to have in-body experiences. For them, out-of-body experiences might be easy, but an escape. Others who are well-grounded could use out-of-body experiences to expand themselves in another direction.

DREAMS

Just as many different trains arrive at the same train station, many different sources communicate with you through your dreams. To understand your dreams, you must view each one individually, not making assumptions about its source. Dreams are often messages from your subconscious. They may also be physical interpretations of something you actually did on the astral plane as you slept. In addition, they could be communications from your essence or guides, alerting you to possible upcoming events that you could avoid. More often than not, dreams are a way of working things out on deeper levels than your conscious mind. Usually, if you "get the message" and deal with those issues consciously, your dreams change.

PYRAMIDS

The pyramids perform several functions. As in literature, a good symbol works on many levels. Their main purpose is to represent the laws of the universe. In doing this, they provide much mathematical information, and focus and transmit energies; their perfect symmetry demonstrates the power that is achieved from true balance.

CREATIVE VISUALIZATION

You will not allow a visualization to work if it would create a situation that is not in keeping with your life plan, or if you are using it to avoid dealing with a present situation.

AFFIRMATIONS

Positive affirmations can be useful. Over time, you can come to genuinely know that what you are affirming is true. However, affirmations will not be successful if you are oblivious to your counterprogramming, unless it is relatively weak. In that case, they can sometimes root it out without your having to deal with it directly.

For example, suppose that you lack prosperity, not because you have a strong negative belief about needing to be in poverty but because it never occurred to you to deliberately create abundance; you think of yourself as only having so much, but that thought is not deeply ingrained. In such a case, affirmations on abundance can work quickly and effectively. On the other hand, if you hold a strong opposing thought, such as "I do not deserve abundance," the affirmation will not "take" until you release the thought.

To give another example, if you affirm, "Life is beautiful and I'm happy," yet you have a strong belief that "Life is a vale of tears and I hate every minute of it," the part of you with the negative belief will see the part of you making the affirmation as a hopeless Pollyanna who is not worth listening to. You will polarize yourself even further than you are now. To release the belief, it may be useful to find out where it came from.

In past-life work, you might discover that there were many experiences that seem to support this belief. Once you see them, you can put them in a larger context, recognizing that it sprang from specific, not universal, occurrences; although painful events sometimes happen, so do beautiful ones. The part of you that is resisting the positive affirmation may then begin to soften. You might enlist it in an experiment to see what happens by taking the attitude that life is beautiful. By deliberately allowing more beauty to come into your life, your belief can begin to change.

Here is an affirmation you may wish to try:

"I am strong and calm enough to handle any situation. I have enough money, time, and energy to do what is needed. I accept my circumstances as starting points and creatively find ways to alter them when possible and necessary."

12 ❊ MASTERY

THE UNIVERSE-ITY

Each person is on a self-study program. You decided what your project would be. You checked it out with your professors, and now have the resources of the entire universe-ity at your disposal. You simply need to learn how to use them.

BEING UNLIMITED

It is hard for most people to conceptualize what being unlimited would be like. We suggest that you confront your limitations one at a time. You will feel increasingly unlimited as you do that.

THE TRUTH

The truth is of the present. If you are willing to see the truth, especially the truth about yourself, it is easier to be in the present. You might say the truth sets you free to be in the present.

KNOWLEDGE

Knowledge is not gleaned from a book. What you know is what you have experienced, what you have made your own through your life. When an idea is truly your own, it is beyond mere intellectual understanding.

As an exercise, you might write down some things you know, as well as some things you intellectually probably understand but do not yet know. You will see that they are different. If a person is on the spiritual path, he aspires to know the things he understands.

It is all right to discuss what you understand and do not yet know, but if you do it too much, your conversation becomes theoretical and lifeless. Others may perceive in you an air of intellectual superiority. Even if you have an excellent intellect, it is wise not to put your purely intellectual understanding center stage. The understanding that carries the most weight is based on knowledge.

SELF-UNDERSTANDING

There is no substitute for conscious self-examination on a regular basis. There are many people in spiritual circles who intellectually are quite knowledgeable but who have not applied much of what they have learned to their own lives. To make an analogy, if you read several books on how to golf but you never swing a club, you are not a golfer. To be truly spiritual, it is necessary to look in the mirror honestly and frequently to see what your actual experience is. This does not mean that you should be self-recriminatory—the essence of spirituality is unconditional love and acceptance, for yourself as well as others—but if you do not even know yourself, how can you love and accept yourself? You do not know what you are accepting. There is little conscious growth without self-examination and complete self-honesty, being humbly willing to acknowledge your shortcomings. If you do not do this, you will still grow, but you will grow the hard way; you will be knocked around. Eventually, you will understand the meaning of your experiences, but it may be several lifetimes down the road. It is much preferable to be awake and know what you are doing now.

CHANGING YOUR BELIEFS

Doesn't changing your beliefs only require willpower?

Willpower is not the best way to describe what is required. It implies that you are imposing something on yourself. It usually does not work very well on deeply entrenched beliefs. Persistence is required, because whatever your beliefs are, they have developed over time. Changing them need not take a long time, but it does take some.

After attending an uplifting, catalytic spiritual gathering, for example, it is common to find yourself falling back into old patterns. You might criticize yourself for this. It is important to recognize that the experience at the gathering was probably just the beginning of a process of change. You have to take responsibility for the change and stay with it if it is to continue. There may be several steps involved. You cannot know ahead of time how long your process will take. Sometimes it takes much longer than you had hoped. The beliefs you are changing may be deep and go back several lifetimes. Nevertheless, you will usually be successful in completing the change if your work is persistent, vigorous, and honest.

If you have self-defeating patterns that do not seem to be changing no matter how much work you do, you may need a fresh approach. It is also possible that change has occurred and you do not see it yet. This is one reason keeping a journal is a good idea. You get a better perspective on where you have been and can see whether change is occurring.

MAINTAINING SPIRITUAL MOVEMENT

I have a lot of spiritual movement when I'm not working, but when I am, I lose it. I reach to other things to give me strength instead of my soul energy, and then I get burned out.

There is great value in integrating the spiritual lessons you learn in your time off with the work you do. We suggest that you begin your days with some sort of meaningful activity, such as taking a quiet walk or writing in your diary, something that helps you connect with your spiritual being. Then, take breaks throughout the day, five or ten minute breathers, to reconnect.

See your work as a meditation itself. Calm your mind so

that it is wholly focused on what you are doing, as if you were meditating while gazing into a flame. This is easier said than done, especially if your work is stressful, but as you practice, you will gain greater facility at it.

If you are still unable to maintain your centering at work, perhaps you should look for a different job in which you might find it easier to have this experience.

THE SPIRITUAL PATH

The spiritual path is not primarily about accumulating information. It is about continually expanding your ability to open, to give and receive, to see, and to handle greater challenges with grace. All of this leads to *agape* [*see glossary*], which is the ultimate transcendent experience.

The spiritual path is often viewed as difficult, the straight and narrow one must tread while trying to avoid temptation. Especially in the beginning, changing defeating habits can be challenging, but in fact, things work better on the spiritual path than they otherwise would. If things are working well, they require less effort, so there is more opportunity to have fun.

You cannot be on the spiritual path and be asleep. However, being awake is not required. Most people are asleep and are experiencing their lessons anyway. They are just experiencing them more painfully and slowly, as a rule, than those who are awake. On the spiritual path, you take responsibility for guiding the course of your life, making intelligent choices rather than functioning automatically. Doing that requires examining the input you receive, both through your own feelings, perceptions, and thoughts, and through other people. Most people do not take adequate advantage of the input they are given, and hence do not make the necessary adjustments to make their lives more pleasing.

We all move in a natural progression, and each step along the way is beautiful. Parents cherish the moments when their little ones take their first steps and speak their first words. It is not better to be twenty-one than one-and-a-half.

Those who are genuinely advanced on the spiritual path see others with compassion and understanding, rather than judging them. This does much to help others grow faster and enjoy their process more.

There are always those who are ahead and those who are behind. However, in a sense, everyone is in the same place because the path is a circle; it has no real beginning or ending.

COMFORT IN THE BODY

What does it indicate if you're uncomfortable being in your body?

Discomfort in your body may indicate that you are not fully in it. You may be resisting the choice that you made to incarnate, or the lessons of your life.

It could also indicate that you are more accustomed to one type of body, and you have chosen to have another type of body in order to find greater balance.

For example, in this era, many people who are more accustomed to a male body are choosing to come into female bodies as a way of learning about the female side of things, and vice versa. Some people prefer the Oriental body and have chosen one that is Caucasian or some other race, and vice versa. Others are accustomed to large, powerful bodies and have chosen to incarnate into small, delicate ones, and vice versa. So discomfort can simply indicate a lack of familiarity: somehow, the body does not seem quite right.

The issue, though, is acceptance, taking responsibility for the choice that you made and learning about your body as much as possible, as you learn about your life.

SUFFERING

Suffering can be a great teacher; for one thing, it can help people to deliberately and consciously choose beauty rather than suffering.

Individual suffering is often self-created; collective suffering has certainly been collectively self-created by humanity. In one sense you could say that suffering is unnecessary, yet in a practical sense it is necessary or it would not exist. When its lessons are learned, it will no longer be necessary. One of the purposes of a spiritual teaching is to show how to reduce and ultimately eliminate suffering. As you expand your ability to love, you reduce your need for suffering.

CRISES

Crises are times of opening. If you could easily handle them from your previous abilities, they would not be crises, and opening would not be required. The fact that they are crises means that you need a larger capacity to handle them, a larger capacity to love.

UNPLEASANTNESS

Some people hope that if they grow enough and eradicate negative beliefs, nothing adverse will ever happen to them again. It's true that life tends to go more smoothly when one is more conscious, but it's not realistic to expect it to be free of unpleasantness. However, as you grow, you have more strength and equanimity, so adversity affects you less.

BUSY-MINDEDNESS

Mental chatter is static. When you are conscious, you broadcast coherently from the station of your mind.

ASKING

To receive of the universe, do not simply ask and then forget about it. There is a constancy to receiving. Stay open, and the response keeps pouring in, a little at a time. Ask, and it is given, but if you ask and then turn your attention away, where can the gift be deposited?

BEING SPIRIT-FULL

Life cannot be spiritual without spirit. An intellectual appreciation of spiritual things is not the same as being spiritual, being of spirit. Spirit has substance to it. It is felt. It is either experienced or it is not. When you focus on a high place, you are filled from that place. Making room within for what is of spirit is the most important part of a spiritual life. One of the ways this is done is through undergoing self-examination and eliminating what is false.

It is much more comfortable to live a spirit-full life. When spirit is missing, it is keenly felt as a void. Those who know of the existence of spirit are the most capable of consciously experiencing it. If you feel spirit in the presence of others who are spirit-full, you can increasingly begin engendering it from within on your own.

COMPLETING THE PHYSICAL PLANE

Many spiritually oriented people hope that their present life will be their last one on the physical plane. The higher planes are easier in some respects, and we do not underestimate the difficulties of the physical plane, but the higher planes have their challenges also. If you have not prepared properly, you can have problems there. As they say, you take yourself with you. Your comfort anywhere has more to do with your inner strength and clarity than any other factor.

The body is sometimes a source of pain, and you do not have to contend with that on higher planes. However, if there are mental or emotional factors behind your pain, you may still be uncomfortable on the astral plane, and find it more difficult to do something about it there. We suggest that you take full advantage of being where you are now, and not turn to spiritual things because you do not like the material world. There is nothing wrong or unspiritual about being on the physical plane. It is not a prison. Many souls actually like it!

Ultimately, each soul decides for itself when it is complete with the physical plane. All is choice. Some think they are finished, only to find out otherwise later. Then they return for another go at it. They may see something incomplete, or an opportunity to be of service that they wish to take advantage of. They may look back at an unsuccessful experience and say, "Let me try that one more time and see if I can do it."

Some souls want to have an in-depth experience of the physical plane. They do not want to miss any important eras or cultures. Others only want to experience the highlights. This is a matter of choice. It is your game. You can play it any way you want to.

Part IV

PERSPECTIVES ON SELF

[To Specific Individuals]

13 ☀ THE BEAUTIFUL SELF

NEEDS

It is well that you are feeling more "selfish." This indicates that you are gaining more respect for the self. True selfishness, as opposed to self-centeredness, is functioning in accordance to the self's needs rather than riding roughshod over them. The self is, in some respects, fragile, and cannot withstand too much abuse. The self is constantly trying to communicate its needs. You are beginning to listen.

May we suggest that you keep a journal of needs that you feel arising in yourself. Just a written acknowledgment of them would be an enormous aid to you. You have been in much denial of them out of your desire to prove that you are not inadequate. Needs are real. If other needs temporarily compromise the filling of personal needs, an imbalance is created that must later be corrected.

PERFECTION

You fear not being perfect. In fact, you are not perfect, at least not in the way you are thinking of it, and will not be for the foreseeable future. Neither are we. We are all moving along, though. And that is perfect.

APPRECIATION

Know within yourself that you are doing the great work you set out to do, and do not lament your lack of perfection. We are not perfect, either, yet you appreciate the value of what we give you. Just so do others, according to their lights, recognize and appreciate the value of your giving to them. Do not underestimate the impact of your life on the people with whom you interact. You are loved and respected by many people.

14 ❋ A HOUSE DIVIDED

PURE EMOTION

Any emotion purely and freely felt is, in its own way, sweet. Inner conflict, like static on a radio signal, can taint it. Grief, for example, when a loved one dies, can be tainted with blaming or doubting yourself. You might wonder if you should have done something different, or think that you are being punished. You might feel guilty about negative feelings toward the one who died. If you can put aside or resolve your conflict about the loss, and experience the pure emotion of grief, it can bring release and healing.

SAFETY

You have built powerful walls around yourself out of an urge for self-protection. They keep out not only harmful forces but also perceptions and useful influences. In recent years, these walls have been wearing thin and in some cases breaking down.

They do not come down overnight. They are coming down at their own pace, and you cannot dictate their dissolution. The inner self lets them be dissolved when you feel safe, and sense that the safety is permanent. Instead of railing at the walls, it would be more productive to focus on creating and expanding safety for yourself.

SELF-JUDGMENT

We suggest that you forget for a while about yourself, your performance, and how others might be judging you. Just be with whatever you are doing. The real problem is that you are judging yourself. You break your developmental flow every time you stop to evaluate how you are doing. These activities have no great purpose in and of themselves, so you can stop worrying about blowing them. Your inner reality is the one that counts. Do not work so hard at that either. Pay attention to it, but without grading it. Love yourself.

FALSE HUMILITY

It is only the false personality that grades and judges. As long as your self-judgment masquerades as humility, you are trapped. Your ruthless torture of yourself is not giving you "brownie points" with "God" or anyone else. This "game" you are playing with yourself allows you to keep your false personality well after you have chased away its more blatant aspects; it looks so "good." We suggest that you be kind to yourself.

COMPARISONS

Do not be afraid of your teacher. Ask him for the help you need. He is really not as unapproachable as you think he is. You just need to approach him as the colleague that he is. He is not better than you are just because he is more experienced, and therefore more capable, in this one area. Had you spent as much time at it as he has, you would be his equal in skill. As it is, you have brought him into your life to teach you something you wish to learn. This does not make him your superior. You are paying for his services. Just because the person at the dry cleaners knows more about dry cleaning than you do, and probably does it much better than you would on your own if you had the necessary equipment, he is not someone you must elevate to a high place in your mental hierarchy. Even if the dry cleaner had an elevated view of himself, you would not have to buy into that.

Each person, no matter how apparently high or low, is valid as he is. He does not have to earn that validity. There is no reason for it other than the simple fact of his being. It was a reality before his first lifetime on this planet, and will continue when the planet is no longer in existence. It is one of the greatest illusions of the physical plane that a person's value can be measured by his achievements, accumulations, or knowledge. The only real reason for achievements, accumulations, or knowledge is that they are useful tools for having a good, creative time while you are here. They are not a measure of the self. All things can be used for good or ill.

If we were going to measure anyone (and we would not be so inclined) we would do it based on the amount of intent one has for the well-being of oneself, others, and the whole. However, we do not know how we would measure that, so we would not even try. Nonetheless, it is evident that you possess mountains of such loving intent. Once you stop feeling that you have to earn your keep on this planet, you will have an easier time just accepting your self-worth as a given and proceeding from that premise.

Human beings often underestimate how long tasks will take. It gives them a good excuse for being impatient or self-deprecating, but that which takes longer often goes deeper and has more staying power. Who can say how long something should take? You keep comparing yourself to other people, and that reinforces your self-deprecation. You are not other people. You are a unique and beautiful spark of the Tao, and so is everyone else. Each person has her own agenda. This is a self-directed curriculum. You are not racing with anyone else. Many other self-deprecating people would feel devastated comparing themselves to you, because you have so much compassion, understanding, and competence in so many ways—but all comparisons of this sort are meaningless.

So what if someone else has an easier time doing something that you are, at the moment, struggling with? That other person is probably struggling somewhere else in his life, even if you cannot see it; if not, there may not be much growth occurring. Even if there is not struggle, and he is growing by leaps and bounds, you do not know what he may have gone through in his previous lifetimes. It might have been a hell that looks ten times worse than yours. You cannot judge these things. The point is that you are doing it in your own way, not in someone else's, and you will do it better if you are not distracted by your judgment of your progress or lack thereof in comparison to that of others. If you know that your path is perfect for you—which it is—you will be less inclined to look at others and envy them their path. The human path is difficult for all. However, there is no advantage to speeding down it as fast as possible. You should go in the way that is best for you, sometimes slow, sometimes fast, sometimes in-between. If you are doing the things in life that most interest you, you do not care how fast you go. You enjoy the process for itself and for the joy of learning.

MASTERING DUALITY

Your task is to master duality. When you are in the waking sleep, dualities master you. You bounce from trying to be a good person to getting angry and being a bad person, back and forth. In mastery, you balance energy so you are neither good nor bad, but appropriate.

Positivity is the "yes" side of things, and negativity, the "no." There are times for both. When they are true and appropriate, they serve the highest good for both yourself and others. Obviously, saying no can sometimes be more constructive than saying yes. "No" can put the brakes on when they need to be on.

Positivity is expansion, and negativity is contraction. Muscles do not merely expand all the time; they expand and contract. That is how there is movement. If everything was always positive in the way you might think of it, there would be no growth.

Those in false positivity, who have frozen smiles on their faces in denial of what is not working in their lives, are unable to put real teeth into making changes because of an investment in seeing only the positive side of things.

Sweetness and light is not necessarily truth.

AVOIDANCE

People often think that if they avoid sorrow, they will have delight. But avoidance is seldom productive.

GUILT

What is guilt?

False guilt is a trickster. It tests you by trying to get you to do things you do not really want to do. If you always knew when it was operating, it would disappear; you would have outwitted the trickster, and that is part of the game.

True guilt provides a useful function. It lets you know when you have violated or hurt another being so you can do something about it and not repeat your error. False guilt tells you that you have done something wrong when you have not actually violated anyone. Both forms of guilt are useful for growth: you grow by overcoming false guilt and by learning from true guilt.

False guilt is far more prevalent than true guilt. If you wish to get rid of false guilt in your life, you must stop accepting the opinions of others as being your final arbiter of truth. You must begin to decide for yourself what a loving action is and what is not. False guilt will not like this, but it will secretly smile to see that you have caught on. The trickster will go bother someone else!

Does true guilt function parallel to karma, so that if you violate another consciousness, you will pay it back?

You will repay karma whether or not you feel guilt. Feeling

guilt may indicate that you understand at least part of the karma's lesson. True guilt also functions in situations that are not karmic but that are still inappropriate. For example, if you unnecessarily speak unkindly to a child and the child cries, this is not a karmic event; you are not going to have to specifically come back and be a child whose elder says something unkind (although you may attract those kinds of experiences). However, true guilt helps you feel for that child.

WANTING

Seek and you shall find. But seek too hard, and what you seek shall elude you. There is a balance in wanting. When you want too much, you are separating yourself from the thing you want. You feel the need to have it so much because you believe that you probably cannot have it. If you simply want something, like wanting an apple that is ripe and ready to be picked from the tree in front of you, you simply reach out your hand and accept it.

15 ❂ HANDLING DIFFICULT EMOTIONS

NAMING PAIN

I f you can name your pain and know it so well that it does not have secret powers over you, you are halfway home.

A GREAT OPPORTUNITY

When you are confused, it is also a time of opportunity, for in dealing with your confusion, you can learn many things that help you to be more effective in all your living.

Difficulties are not "bad." They may simply be evidence of growth occurring against the resistance of blocks. You do not usually notice your growth until you come up against something that impedes it. The block has no doubt been there all along. You can be thankful that you are now aware of it, because that awareness gives you the possibility of eliminating it and thereby lightening your load.

FEAR

There are hazards on the physical plane that deserve caution. Fear is a mechanism by which a red flag goes up, so that if it is wise to draw away, you are alerted. Otherwise, you might blindly wander into dangers you are not equipped to handle.

The more evolved the soul, the more capable it is of handling the challenges of the physical plane and the less fear that is needed. When there is complete mastery, there is no fear, but of course, this is a very rare achievement. Spiritual mastery results in *agape*, or unconditional love. Jesus said that perfect love casts out fear. When there is *agape*, there is no need for fear.

On higher planes, fear is virtually eliminated, by both the increased progress toward *agape* and the absence of hazards.

Still, between lives people often carry with them a measure of their physical plane fear, partly out of habit, although this is reduced as there is a relaxation of attachment to the prior lifetime.

A little bit of fear goes a long way. As with so many things on the physical plane, the use of fear is unnecessarily and harmfully disproportionate to its need.

If you are on the spiritual path, there is a steady reduction of fear. If you are not less fearful, it might be wise to question how well you are recognizing and validating the lessons of the path. If fear is the motivation for seeking the path in the first place, progress is limited until this desire for avoidance is replaced, at least somewhat, by an enjoyment of the positive rewards of the path. They include greater self-confidence, a lessening of divisiveness, both internal and external, and a more expansive camaraderie with others, stemming from an increased identification with all humanity. These steps, of course, relate to the great goal, *agape*.

How can you reduce fear?

Look at your fear as directly as possible. Get to know it, rather than running from it. If you look at your fear lovingly, it will most likely tell you its story, and once its story is told, it will begin to dissipate. Because it is a messenger, it needs to do its job and deliver its message. If you allow it to do that, it will be happy, and it will eventually dissolve back into the love force from which it came. All things come from love.

You cannot be certain whether to advance or retreat in the face of fear without going into the fear. Usually, when you go through your fear and come out the other side, you feel impelled to advance, but maybe differently than you had originally planned. In listening to your fear, you are receiving insight about some possibly valid concerns that might help you modify your approach.

For example, suppose that you want to bring a subject to someone's attention, but you are afraid of his reaction. You know that he has a bad temper, low self-esteem, or whatever. When the fear arises, you might first question whether you wish to proceed at all, but in giving it some thought, you come up with a diplomatic way of saying what you need to that is effective and unlikely to trigger a negative reaction. In that way, the fear assisted you in protecting both yourself and the other person. In continuing to listen to your fear, you might discern that its excess charge is related to painful experiences with other people. As you work through them, your loving and reassuring listening helps neutralize it, allowing you to approach this person more calmly.

Anything you want a great deal generates a similar amount of fear. If you want something that much, you view having it as being a long way from where you are. It is like attempting a long jump in track that is farther than you have done before—it is natural to feel some fear. Your fear can help you gather your energy to achieve this jump. There are many actors who say that they would be concerned if they did *not* have butterflies before going onstage. The butterflies assist them in giving their best performance. If, however, the butterflies are excessive, they can be debilitating. This has to do with the way you interpret the fear. It becomes debilitating when it triggers false beliefs, such as, "After all, I'm inadequate. I can't do this. What if such-and-such happens?" If your interpretation instead is, "This is a big stretch and I know I can do it," which is more likely to be the truth, you may reach new heights.

When your inner self comes forth, you are alive and powerful. Fear of aliveness and power can be major obstacles to letting your inner self come forth. False fear reasons, "If I am too alive, others might not like me. If I am too powerful, I may misuse that power." When you let your inner self come forth, your fears begin to dissolve.

I have a fear of heights. I can go to the top of a tall building, but I can't be out on an open cliff. How can I distinguish whether it is true, valid fear or something from the past?

A fear of heights or any phobia is usually a result of a past-life trauma. You probably fell from a cliff or some other height. If something traumatic happens to you, you tend to fear that it will happen again until you deal with it. Just clearly recognizing the cause can help reduce if not eliminate the fear. You might wish to undergo past-life regression to see under what circumstances you fell and get a vivid picture of the fact that that threat is no longer in your life.

How can you tell if you are afraid because of a past life or because you don't want to deal with something in the present?

These two factors are intimately related. Why do you not wish to deal with something? There was probably something in the past that made you afraid of dealing with it. Most fear relates to the past in some way. It does not matter whether that past was earlier in this life or in a past life; it is all the past.

If there is something in your present circumstance that you do not wish to deal with, such as a bad relationship, then the question is, "What am I afraid will happen if I deal with this? Losing the relationship? If I lose the relationship, what else will I lose? Will I lose financially, or whatever? Suppose that I lose financially. Does that mean I will be destitute? If I'm destitute, does that mean that I will die from starvation?" If you follow out your thinking, you might find that your real fear in confronting the issue is that you will die of starvation as you did in a past life.

If you know that there is something that you do not want

to deal with and have the courage to deal with it anyway, you might seek outside assistance so that it will be less threatening and you can be more effective.

Fear causes you to draw away, whereas love seeks to blend.

DOUBT

What do you gain from all your doubting? We suggest that you take a moratorium on doubting for a month. It is so habitual that you cannot discriminate when doubt is really called for.

Ask yourself instead, "What do I know?" You may find that you have more clarity than you acknowledge. Your doubt and confusion are largely a smoke screen. You are afraid to own what you know partly because that would require you to take responsibility for your actions, which in turn would give others a clear shot to criticize you. It is safe to take responsibility for your life and for your decisions.

ANGER

Those whose anger is destructive do not have mastery of it. Anger is simply opposing, outward-thrusting energy. Working with your anger teaches you greater mastery of your life force. When you allow anger to move properly in the face of danger, it protects you; it is your strength coming forth to keep harm away. All energy seeks movement. When anger is not allowed to move, it gathers and builds pressure against what is blocking it. Something has to give, so it seeks any way it can to get out. When you become angry in the present, your excess anger from the past may want to come through as well.

Does all anger have pain beneath it?

Not necessarily. Anger can also be based in frustration: you want to do something, but have not found a way that works properly. The answer to this type of anger is to slow down, size up the situation, and either change your tactics or stop trying to do something that cannot be done at that time, if that is the case. But most anger, particularly rage, is sourced in pain, or fear of pain based on past pain.

The ability to be angry is healthy. A person with no capacity for anger is a person with a broken spirit. If you cannot be angry, you are saying to the world, "I do not deserve protection. You can do something terrible, and I will just accept that."

There is a record of Jesus expressing anger toward money changers. When he spoke on another occasion about turning the other cheek, perhaps he was referring to not resisting attack or reacting combatively. When you resist, it hits you harder; when you react combatively, you intensify the conflict. If someone attacks you, it is better to neutralize his energy. A skilled martial artist can move an attacker's energy past him so that it does not hit him, using it to put the attacker on his back.

Sometimes a more gentle and kind approach can neutralize an attacker's energy, but that is not the same as being passive or without anger. At its core, anger is the intent to maintain boundaries, whether this is done constructively or destructively. Constructive anger is loving, whether it is expressed gently or forcefully, because it is concerned with the highest good. When you are angry constructively, you take necessary action with strength but also with as little harm as possible. This requires being careful and conscious; the more power you are dealing with, the more damage you can do if you misuse it, but many times, action does need to be taken. If you witness someone violating the sanctity of another individual and have the capacity to do something about it, your anger can empower you to appropriate, effective action. If you use your anger insensitively, you just have a fight on your hands. This is not the purpose of anger in the larger scheme.

Anger is like the mythical dragon in his lair who pops out spontaneously. It's not easy to deal with it rationally. This is especially true if you have not had much practice in expressing it appropriately and have a large backlog.

When the dragon arises, you can be grateful: it is your personal power. However, when you first get to know him, he is unruly. You have kept him chained in the basement without food and water and he is not very cooperative. You need to get him out in the fresh air and let him run around, kick and squeal, and safely burn down a tree or two so that an entire forest is not destroyed. In other words, you need to release your old anger. When you do, your personal power is a stable and strong fire burning within you rather than one that swells up and then dies off.

When you react toward someone beyond what is warranted in that situation, old anger is probably being triggered. The fact that it is near the surface indicates that you are ready to work through it. The first step is to release the pent-up energy that you are holding in your body.

To do so, we suggest that you take fifteen minutes every day to be alone in a private place. You can pound, jump, hit, or stamp—whatever comes naturally to your body once you get it started. Be forceful but safe, using pillows or other soft surfaces to cushion the blows. Also say whatever words or make whatever sounds that come up. If you are in a place that is not soundproof and you wish to scream, you can do it into a pillow to muffle the noise. Be sure to keep your throat open and relaxed so you do not hurt your voice.

In the beginning at least, you might want to have a friend or therapist with you who understands the value of emotional release. He can help provide a safe place for you, supporting and coaching you in staying conscious and in control.

Continue until you feel emptied out for the day, but if it starts to feel like it is getting beyond your safety level, or if it has gone much beyond fifteen or twenty minutes, stop. Then contemplate what came up. Do not judge it, though; although anger obviously can take a destructive form, its existence itself is always valid. After a while, you will have accumulated a lot of understanding of the roots of your anger.

Your unresolved anger comes out toward your children because you are afraid to direct it toward adults. Your children are "safe" for you because they cannot fight back very much. As you learn to express it with appropriateness and effectiveness, you will feel stronger in your own power, and will have less of a need to dump it in the wrong places. You will know that with whomever you are angry, you can resolve it directly.

Suppose that you find in your "basement," left over from your childhood, a lot of anger toward your mother because she used to make fun of you. As a canny player of the game of life, you might say, "Anger—that is energy just sitting down there in my basement, not being used. I'm going to clean it up so I can use it." You might then "bring it upstairs" and express it in a safe, perhaps therapeutic environment, so it can come free of its old pattern and again manifest as pure energy. That gives you more energy and understanding with which to play the game.

The energy formed the pattern called "anger" for a good reason: it was seeking to protect you from being hurt by your mother's insensitivity and lack of understanding when you were a child. However, it never got to do its job. You had to hold it in because it was not safe for you at the time to express it.

Rather than releasing anger, sometimes people criticize themselves for having it: "I really should not be angry at my mother. After all, that was thirty years ago. I'm a grown adult. She's such a sweet little old lady. I would not want to hurt her feelings." Or, "After all, I chose my parents—I am to blame," so the anger is turned inward. This attitude would not aid you in winning the game. The fact is that you have anger in the basement. You are either going to use it to win the game or you are going to let it sit there.

The problem with letting it sit there is that it tends to cry out for attention until it is released, because all energy seeks union with the whole. Energy does not like being kept in little separate boxes. So if you are being practical about it, you say, "I'm going to see what this anger has to teach me. It is there, after all. It's there whether I acknowledge it or not, whether I act upon it or not."

When you release and integrate it, you might begin to remember past-life experiences that relate to it, such as one in which you were placed in the center of the square and ridiculed and stoned for your beliefs, and died. If you had this ultimate experience of belittlement, there would likely be a part of you that fears that if you are belittled, you will die. This fear would have increased your anger at your mother's belittlement, because you felt that you were struggling for your life. Now that you are more consciously aware of the fear behind your anger, you can begin to release both your fear and anger by listening to and comforting the part of you that experienced violation. You can bring to bear the knowledge that in that life, you did die from having different beliefs, but that now your life is not threatened by this and you will not die if you are belittled. You no longer need that fear and anger to keep you safe.

Something may also need to be said to your mother, both to honor your feelings and so that she can grow and learn from your experience, too. In any case, you can affirm that no matter what anyone else says or does, you love and support yourself. You need not accept the belittlement of others anymore.

You may have internalized the belittlement of others and hence belittle yourself, perhaps hoping that if you do it first, others will not. You can decide that you no longer need to be involved in any form of belittlement.

One person can use his childhood as an excuse for being miserable, and another can use his to help him win the game. From going through a process like the one we just described, you can become more compassionate, wise, understanding of yourself and others, and skilled at handling life's challenges. You would tend to attract much less belittlement from others, if that was your story, and if you did attract it, you would know better how to handle it.

Can you get someone who makes house calls to clean your basement?

You have to clean your own basement! If you got someone else to do it, he would get all the lessons and growth, and you would be mad about that. You would say, "I went through all of those difficult experiences, and you are going to collect the knowledge and understanding from them. That's not fair!" It sounds very tempting to call in a cleaning service to hose down your subconscious mind, but it would not work.

You seem to believe that if you express your anger in an inappropriate way just once, everyone around you will crumble, and it will be all your fault. That belief is based in a past life in which your wrath was indeed highly destructive, and you learned something from that. However, do not throw the baby out with the bath water. What looks like inappropriate anger to you may in fact be the kick in the pants that someone needs. As you lose your fear of your power, it is easier to handle it appropriately.

When you lose your temper, you lose control; you are reacting. When you allow your inner self to come forth, you act with power and are in control. Hence, you do not need to react. Your actions may look similar to those that are reactive, but you are simply doing what is necessary in that situation.

In your culture, you are taught conflicting things about anger. It is seen as being more appropriate for men to be angry than for women, but it is generally felt that nice people do not become angry. It is true that nice people are angry appropriately, but in the face of a cruel and violent threat to life, for instance, your ability to freely express a large amount of force could make the difference between surviving or not, so it is good to have that capacity wide open.

If you have a lot of blocked anger, and your inhibitions are broken when someone attacks you, the force of it coming forth might be very powerful, but it will probably not be in control. You might do unnecessary harm both to him and yourself. So it is better to move your blocked anger out ahead of time.

He who has true strength has the ability to be truly gentle, because he has confidence in his ability to use his force, not necessarily physical force, to protect himself when necessary. He does not have to keep a guard up. People who are always showing off their strength are insecure about it.

HATE

If you hate your hate, you have more hate.

Fear is the opposite of love, not hate.

Some people numb themselves because they are afraid of dealing with their hate. To come fully to love, sometimes it is necessary to know your hate. There are many cruel people who apparently know their hate, but they do not really, because hate can only be known by love.

The hate and destruction that have dominated much of

history results from the denial of it. We doubt that Hitler or Stalin would have admitted their hatred. They would probably have claimed that they were bettering humanity.

If you know your hate, you understand what is behind it. You have consciousness about it. Hate does not rule you. If you have hated in the past, there was a reason for it. Knowing your hate can bring you increased understanding, and understanding leads to love. Love is not complete until it has found understanding, not necessarily intellectual understanding, but knowing. Love knows itself, and everything is ultimately love.

Hate is energy seeking to push away what is harmful, or what appears to be harmful. When you transform it into love, you feel safe, because love has its own native strength to handle whatever arises.

RELEASE

I've been having strong reactions to a particular situation. As I explore them, I realize that they are connected to unresolved issues of the past, and I begin to doubt their validity in relation to the present.

Although you may be overreacting based on unresolved issues of the past, part of your response may also be valid in relation to the present. By first releasing and working through your excess reaction, you can better make an appropriate response to the situation.

There is the potential here for a large release. Blocks preventing ecstasy can become bridges into it when you let your energy move the blocks.

PRIMING THE PUMP

I seem to have a lot of storms going on within me recently that I'd like to understand better.

When you prime a pump, you first draw out the stale water that has been sitting in the pipes; fresh, clean water follows. You are activating your emotions, and those that most need healing are coming up first. Some of them relate to your movement toward increased self-respect. You are learning to act in ways that indicate your value to yourself. This is helping flush out feelings of unworthiness.

LAYERS OF EMOTIONS

There are usually many layers to deep emotional hurts, many of them relating to past lives. Underneath a feeling of anger might be a feeling of having been betrayed. Underneath that may be the belief that "I'm not good enough. That's why I was betrayed." The reason you do not feel good enough is because of something that you did that you still feel guilty about. And so forth.

The more these things become conscious, the easier it is to heal them, although it is not always necessary to make every aspect of an emotional hurt conscious. There are certain central pieces that, when understood, pull up and heal many other pieces that are attached to them. The aim is to discover the core of the hurt. You cannot always reach it in the beginning. You may have to peel away one layer at a time.

Begin with the recognition that all your feelings are good. Everyone has at one time or another been taught that at least some, if not all, of his feelings are invalid: "You shouldn't feel that way. Of course your mother and father love you," for example. If you feel that your parents do not love you, you *should* feel that way. There is a good reason you feel that way, whether or not your feeling is objectively accurate. If you accept the validity of all your feelings, you have a starting point for going into them. You can approach them with the understanding that they have something to teach you. We suggest that you love and listen to all your feelings.

There is an aspect of everyone that feels murderous, for instance. We are not suggesting that it is appropriate to murder someone because you feel murderous, but the feeling is valid. It has something to say.

Suppose that you therapeutically release some rage about something that happened when you were five years old; you beat pillows as hard as you can and then collapse, exhausted. You feel wonderful because something you had been sitting on has been allowed to come forth. But that is not the end of the process. It was probably the scab on top of the wound. Now you can begin to tune in more subtly to what was underneath, letting those things come out, understanding them with compassion. It keeps going deeper. You might begin to have past-life memories surface.

We do not wish to imply that such a process is necessarily lengthy and tedious. Sometimes these steps can be passed through quickly. The more skill you or your counselor has in working with the process, the more quickly you can move through the different steps that are required. When you feel completely neutral about what had previously troubled you, you are done—for now, anyway. You may find that other layers are not ready to come forth and heal at this time. What you let go of is all the fruit that is ripe enough, so to speak, to fall from the tree.

This process has much value, not just from the standpoint of getting rid of something, but of acquiring wisdom. You are getting to know a part of yourself that has always been there. You are not getting rid of the experiences that were hurtful; you are transforming them into growth. You are integrating them into yourself. As traumas, they are lessons in hermetically sealed boxes. They are there, but they have no benefit to you because you do not really know what is inside. Healing them is opening the boxes.

VALUING EMOTIONS

Your neck problem comes from your tendency over many lives to not face your emotions. You store the unresolved emotions in your neck, which places a burden on it. It stiffens and goes out. The reason you do not face your emotions is that you do not think they are very important. You think that getting the job done is the important thing. We are not underestimating the importance of getting the job done, but you underestimate the importance of emotions in getting the job done. If you had been in greater touch with your feelings, you might have been able to sense your partner's dishonesty and avoid being cheated, for example.

Obviously, your wife is much more oriented in her emotions than you are. You think it is because she is a woman but that is only partly true. She tends to be more in touch emotionally even in her male lifetimes. Part of her agreement with you is to teach you about your emotions. Never assume that what she or even your baby daughter is feeling is irrational. Listen closely for the truth of what is there. Try to understand it.

Whenever you have a glimmer of emotional response to a situation, talk with her about it. Let yourself cry if you want to. It may take some time before deep emotions start coming up, but when they do, let yourself feel them. You will notice a marked improvement in your neck. This will take time, so be patient.

We are not saying that you should become a highly emotional person. You never will be, because that is not your nature. Your primary nature is to do, and you do "doing" well. Just do not be at an extreme. Let yourself experience other parts of yourself. This includes some emotion and introspection. Including these other elements will help you feel more integrated.

DETACHING FROM FEELINGS

Opening to feelings is essential. The next step is to feel and at the same time have detachment from the feelings. Be the feelings and the one who is feeling them, and the one who is watching the one who is feeling them, if you can.

Feelings are like children who want their mommy to understand more about them than they understand about themselves. If your three-year-old daughter comes to you crying because her knee was skinned when she fell down, if you begin crying along with her, also thinking that this skinned knee is the equivalent of a leg amputation, then you are not really doing too much to console your daughter. Let the "daughter" part of you cry and feel the feeling as you take her in your arms, clearly see the problem, and help make it better. Do not make her wrong for her crying, dismissing it as "only a skinned knee." Let her know that everything is going to be all right.

WHATEVER YOU ARE FEELING

Whatever you are feeling in the moment needs your highest respect and less editing on your part. You do not have to conform to model behavior as defined by others. A less narrow view of what is appropriate would be helpful.

BALANCE

There is a balance in all this. You do not need to spend every waking hour dealing with your emotions. At some point, your child within needs to be sent out to play. You can only do so much emotional work at one time, just as you can only do so much physical, mental, and spiritual work at one time.

All life seeks balance. There are times to think, to feel, and to act. There are times to be silly and to be serious. There are times to work on yourself and to serve others. It can be hard to find this balance. Noticing which part of yourself feels the most neglected can help make you aware of where balance lies for you now.

16 ❖ WORKING WITH YOURSELF

FINDING YOURSELF

Finding yourself is a gradual process. There is no substitute for the full living of each day. As you uncover the falsities that cover you from the view of the world and yourself, you will be more and more evident. It is likely that you are already more present than you realize. Others can probably see your beauty better than you can. That is because the "squeaky wheels" of your unresolved inner conflicts are getting the grease of your attention. The parts of you that are already in order do not seem to warrant concern. One way to cultivate a more balanced view is to make a list of all the beautiful qualities you already possess, and read it daily.

GENERATING CLARITY

You are merely suffering from a lack of focus. We suggest that you make a detailed list for each situation that has been difficult, with two headings: one, everything you know that is true about it; and two, everything concerning it about which you still feel unresolved. This will help you get some of the swirl out of your mind. It is difficult to assimilate everything at once; if you "divide," you can "conquer." Also, your thoughts will be safely down on paper. Therefore, you will not feel compelled to think about the situations constantly in order to avoid forgetting them.

You can write the first list as statements, and the second as questions. Make the questions as clear and penetrating as possible. It is not important to come up with answers at this point. "Ask, and it shall be given to you." When you are clear on what you want resolved, your inner reality can set upon the task of generating answers. Your inner reality is wise and resourceful. Trust that after whatever time is required, answers will be there. There is no need to keep asking, although you can revise your lists as often as you like. The more clarity you bring to them, the more clarity will come as a result.

Each day, review your lists and record any answers you have received, checking off the questions that you now feel you have clarity on. If an answer is only partial, rephrase the question to cover the parts still unanswered.

Be a "hog"—you can have as much clarity as you wish. You can ask as many questions of reality as you like, and reality will not mind a bit. Other people may not have patience with a "nitpicking" list of questions, but your own reality is willing to take them all on.

This process will remove much of the confused stress from your body. You will be able to relax because all that raw material for research will now be safely organized in a form that your internal computer can digest, and the solving of your problems will be set in motion. When problems are pressing on you strongly, you want resolution immediately, but when you know that you are handling them, it is easier to be patient and have the necessary detachment to deal with them. Your inherent ability to love will flourish when the burden of trying to deal with everything at once is removed.

CHANGING YOUR LIFE

To help you find clarity, we recommend that you make three lists. Be as specific as possible, but you can also include general attributes.

First, list the things you feel good about in your life. Remember to include supportive relationships, material possessions, knowledge, memories, and so on—anything that is positive for you.

Next, list the things that you would like to be different. Be specific.

Finally, list the things that you want to create in your life of a positive nature. Affirm that you can have those things, and that you are willing to do what is required to create them. Let it be fun for you, like a child filling out his list for Santa Claus, but do not worry about when Christmas will come for you. Just remember that the clearer you are about what you want to create in your life, the more likely it is that you will create it. If you create something that almost fits the bill but is missing something, add what is missing to the list.

Keep refining your lists, making them more specific and changing them as you become clearer about your life and what you want.

TO SOMEONE SEVENTY-FIVE YEARS OLD

Those who have matured physically are often more spiritually full. Hence, a greater breadth of spiritual intercourse may occur through the increased activation of your essence. These may truly be golden years. All the earlier lessons and experience of life can be integrated. As you further nurture your connection with your essence, you will find that all you do is thereby enriched.

Much is internalized through external action for you. While working, lessons on which you have been meditating can root. It is, therefore, valuable for you to begin your days in contemplation, even if only for a few minutes. You might, for instance, decide upon a quality that you wish to increase in the day ahead of you, such as peace or relaxation. Put this in the back of your mind. Then throughout the day be aware of it coming through. At the end of the day, take a few moments and see how your experience has grown in that day. This requires no effort or struggle. It is merely a matter of gently opening to what is already there. The story of the tortoise and the hare is applicable. One who grows a little each day has real and lasting benefits.

17 ❈ CHOICES

LESSONS

Lessons learned under such adverse situations are never forgotten, so do not regret your choices. You have forever to enjoy the fruits of your difficult labors.

PRIORITIES

You cannot make any wrong decisions. There is no need to worry about the things you do not get done. You have all of forever to get to them. Just keep reevaluating what your highest priorities truly are.

We suggest that you take short breaks throughout the day to relax and check in with yourself. Ask what the most balancing activity would be. It might be quiet time, exercise, socializing, work, or something else. Follow through on it as soon as you can.

DECISIONS

You have important work to do in this life. Your choices are not inconsequential to the larger family of mankind. On the other hand, you cannot make a "wrong" choice. Whatever you decide will lead to a valuable growth experience, and will prepare you for what is to come. However, the choices that will bring the most benefit and joy are generally those that are aligned with your true desires.

You feel pressed to make a choice soon. This comes from a habit of giving power to others. It is your life. If you are not ready to decide, you do not have to. Give yourself the gift of honoring your own process.

It is good to give thought to the pros and cons surrounding each choice, but you can take this to an extreme. Do not allow your mind to try to hurry up your heart. At some point, you have to put down the arguments pro and con, and wait until you know. It would be useful to you to write down all of the pros and cons in your decision-making, because if you get them on paper, you will put them out of your mind and be able to be more objective about them.

Because you live on the physical plane and there are logistics involved, it sometimes takes time to manifest what you most want and need, but this does not mean you cannot have it. Do not assume that having what you want and need must be difficult. You can have anything you want if you are willing to do what is required to have it. If you are not, then perhaps you do not want and need it all that much. When you have given your heart time to know, you may realize that some of the things you thought you wanted and needed are not really that important to you. Because you have allowed yourself your process, you will feel that you have clarified rather than compromised.

SOLUTIONS

What is most constructive for you is also most constructive for the whole, including the others in your life. There is no conflict between the individual and the whole. If you think there is, you probably have not yet accurately perceived what is best for you. There may be another solution, slightly different from what you had thought of, that would truly be the best for all. Do not give up if you have not yet found it.

By the same token, what you truly want is never at the expense of what someone else truly wants. Both can be accommodated. You need not worry about being too selfish.

KEEP IT MOVING

The things you do not want in your life will be wanted by someone else, so let them keep moving and stay with what you want.

18 ☀ ACHIEVEMENT

ACCOMPLISHMENTS

You tend to be hard on yourself regarding your lack of accomplishments. Yes, a certain amount of accomplishment is valid and necessary for you, but remember that your life is more concerned with being.

It is more difficult to do anything well under the burden of anxiety. Your efforts to shed this are most valuable.

MOVEMENT

It may appear that things are moving slowly, but remember, movement can be either horizontal, from A to B, or vertical, from A down to a deeper level of A. When that deeper A moves to B, you have moved a much larger volume of material than if you had moved from A to B across the surface of your being.

OBSTACLES

If you give up every time you hit obstacles, eventually you begin to get tired of that and choose to become creative in finding ways around them.

TRY AND TRY AGAIN?

When you keep repeating an unsuccessful experience, you may be unwittingly reinforcing the blocks instead of letting them go. There is a fine line here, and only you can know if you are on the verge of a breakthrough or a breakdown!

The willingness to see both options (quitting or sticking with it) as possible means of reaching your goals will help you be more neutral about the issue and make a better decision.

EXPERIMENTS

Living is like a research project. You can always try another experiment if one does not work. That is how Edison invented the light bulb.

19 ☀ AFFIRMING LIFE

THE MEANING OF LIFE

Sometimes people feel futile, that their lives are not going anywhere, and they passively wait for its meaning to emblazon itself across the sky of their consciousness. However, if your life seems to have no meaning, it is because you yourself have not given it one.

SUICIDE

Most suicides are choices made by the personality against the wishes of her essence, and are often karmic because of the extreme blow to those left behind. There are better ways of dealing with great problems. Going so massively against the grain of one's being is not comfortable, to say the least. In general, when the personality chooses to follow a different course from what her essence would like, it can be painful, but sometimes it leads to much growth and new discoveries. A suicide, however, is almost always ill-advised, and creates more problems than it solves. Even so, no choice is "bad," and after one or two suicides most learn for themselves that it is preferable to face their problems.

TO SOMEONE CONSIDERING SUICIDE

You came here for many good reasons, not all of them for your own growth. You play on many "teams" in order to accomplish various larger goals. You are an important participant. If you were not where you are, doing what you do, that spot would be vacant. No one can replace you. You are unique and special. Taking your life would be a tremendous waste and setback. You know too much, are too full of as yet unexplored potential, to throw it down the drain.

You think you are being logical and rational in your choice-making process, but your illusions effectively block perception and make illogical thinking look logical. There is also a certain amount of laziness here. We are not suggesting that you crack the whip against yourself either, to continually make yourself do undesirable things. That is false discipline, being motivated by fear. You are coming out of that. You are not yet adequately motivated by love, which is true discipline. Love impels you to do things that ultimately bring the greatest blessing and joy to yourself and others. Since you are in between these two motivations, you tend to lack motivation altogether, and laziness is the result.

Doing what you love is not the same as doing what you like. What you love includes a sense of higher purpose, a need you gladly fulfill because of the good it can do for all. Some activities are less pleasant than others, but if they are necessary to this higher purpose, you do them. This is the nature of *agape*, or unconditional givingness. Of course, sometimes you can find creative ways to have others do things that you do not care to do, by paying for a service or bartering, for instance. This makes sense when it is possible, but life is not about always being comfortable.

Those who are rich and do not have to lift a finger sometimes feel the same malaise as you do. The issue is not what you think it is. It is not about having to work to earn a living. It is about feeling part of the world, being an active participant in it. Those who "march to a different drummer" can have an especially difficult time feeling a sense of community with the world. Can you acknowledge that your premises in life are different from those of most others, yet also acknowledge the common denominators, namely your humanity and your desire to move more deeply into the light?

You are not in denial by doing something that is not your favorite thing to do unless you deny that it is not your favorite thing to do. If it is done honestly in the knowledge that it seems necessary to do it and that you have not yet found another way for it to be done without your direct participation, there will be no loss or damage to yourself from the act. Being a loving and compassionate parent to yourself, you might then treat yourself to something nurturing.

There is more indulgence in your personality than will ultimately serve your higher purposes. Indulgence is a form of escape, whereas self-nurturing brings you more fully into the present. You might do the same activity to nurture as to indulge, but nurturing is conscious, carefully tended and a beautiful experience, whereas indulgence is unconscious, like an alcoholic binge, and leaves you with a sense of emptiness following it.

Doing just what you want, when you want to do it, is not really an exercise in choice making. It is not treating the moment as a new one, freshly evaluating it for what would be the highest possible action. It is an act of laziness guided by automatic pilot. Mind you, the highest possible choice may be to do what you would also do on automatic pilot, but you would likely execute it slightly differently when your consciousness is present to guide it, and the result would feel different.

It is difficult to grow up in a world that is not aligned with your needs. You are always going to be a little out of step. Fortunately, you have the insight and wisdom, if you choose to use it, to work within the existing structure and make a basically comfortable and happy place in it for yourself. It will require work, but contrary to your belief system, the right type of work will make you happy, and in fact, you cannot be happy without it.

COMFORT

Being uncomfortable with something is not the same thing as being inadequate to do it. Comfort is largely a matter of familiarity.

THE PURSUIT OF JOY

You advised me to pursue joy to a greater extent, and I was wondering if there are any qualifications on that? There are a lot of things you can do to make yourself feel joyous: get drunk, take crack, engage in sexual pleasures, sky dive, fish, and so on. What limitations do you place on the pursuit of joy, if any?

There is a difference between joy and pleasure, or at least, false pleasure. There are experiences that you are conditioned to find pleasurable, but actually experience as violations. The limit to the pursuit of pleasure is what causes harm to yourself or others. Joy results from harmony with the whole, so it needs no limits.

The way people eat illustrates well the difference between joy and pleasure. Most people eat for pleasure. Few people eat for joy. Of course, some people eat for neither one, but just to survive. When you eat for pleasure, you are usually not that aware of what you are eating. The food functions more or less as a drug; it pacifies you and stimulates certain of your senses, but you do not really experience it. When you eat for joy, you focus your awareness on what you are eating, almost as a form of meditation. You choose food that best harmonizes with your body, and this also makes it highly satisfying.

SPONTANEITY

What is called spontaneity can simply be automatic pilot at work. True spontaneity is creating something fresh, with the full presence of your faculties of alertness and choice-making. For example, someone who improvises at the piano on automatic pilot puts together fragments of music he remembers from the past and uses familiar chord progressions; the music rambles, without shape. Someone who improvises with true spontaneity is conscious and sensitive; he continually scans possible choices and selects those that feel best. Of course, he would have to have had much practice and probably study to gain the necessary musical skills and vocabulary. The greater they are, the more accomplished his improvising will be.

To develop your "vocabulary" for living spontaneously, take time out regularly to consider your choices. The more options you are aware of in handling situations, the less you take for granted, and the more effectively you can "improvise."

BEING CAREFREE

It is a beautiful thing to be carefree. Children can often teach adults much about it. The adult view is usually that it is impossible to be carefree. One has responsibilities, after all: bills to pay and problems to deal with. But you do not have to lose the abilities you had when you were a child; ideally, they grow as you do, but if they didn't in the past, you can now relearn to be carefree.

HAPPINESS

Happiness is not, contrary to popular belief, the absence of troubles. Happiness is seeing clearly what is beautiful in life while also seeing clearly whatever troubles you have. When you see both, you can effectively handle your troubles. You can take care of them, work around them, or make peace with them. If you do not have a clear understanding of what is beautiful in life, you have no basis from which to heal your troubles. When you use what is right and beautiful in your life to handle them, they look different. You see them as merely raw material for developing your mastery of life. A master can handle whatever troubles arise with love, truth, and no damage to his own well-being or that of others. Therefore, he is able to be consistently happy. You have constant opportunities to develop such mastery. If you are learning a musical instrument, you will play plenty of wrong notes before your Carnegie Hall debut. That is to be expected. But if you keep practicing, your skills improve.

Each person needs time focused on the beautiful in life: a walk in the park, buying something simply because you like it and it gives you pleasure, staying in the bathtub even when you have work to do, or making your work environment more beautiful and pleasant for yourself.

Meditate on what is good in your life and write it down. Thank everyone in your life, physical and nonphysical, as well as all the parts of yourself, for all they have brought to you. Thank every one of your circumstances, too. Everything in your life has given you raw material for increasing your happiness.

If you try to force yourself to be happy all the time before you are, you will succeed only in lying to yourself. However, the genuine experience of happiness is available, and although it cannot be forced, it can be allowed.

A LIGHTER VIEW

You sometimes take things far too seriously. That is hazardous to your growth!

It is important not to let the mundane aspects of life dominate.

ENJOYMENT

Each day is available for your enjoyment.

You would do well to develop a capacity for enjoyment that does not hinge on everything going flawlessly.

You need to have more fun. No one can give you this; you must give it to yourself. Decide what is fun for you and then pencil it into your schedule book. Honor it as if it were an appointment with an important client. Do things in which you move: a bicycle ride on a lovely spring day, for example. Buy yourself flowers and express your delight and surprise at receiving such beautiful flowers from someone you love!

KNOWING

Your greatest treasure is your knowing. Knowing is the source of your power. When you possess your power, you live in abundance. Honor your knowing. You have much, but you sometimes make little of it.

Part V

FOLLOWING THE PATH

20 ❋ TRANSCENDENCE AND SELF-KNOWLEDGE

It is good to take stock, to know where you are at any given time. People, like stores, often do a yearly inventory around the first of the year, making resolutions. This may be often enough for a store, but it is probably not enough for you.

There is a transcendent knowledge available to each person. What is transcendence? It could be defined as simply rising high enough to see what is going on.

Suppose that you are a mechanic repairing a part in a piece of equipment. You are focused on this aspect of the whole. When you are done, you test the equipment; you step back and look at its entire operation to see whether the part is fixed. Similarly, if you are a sculptor working in stone, you stand far enough away to see the whole piece in perspective. After due deliberation you come up close and chisel a piece away. Then you step back again and see how it looks.

It is rare for people to do this with their lives. They tend to be occupied with details. Those in poverty are occupied with survival. People who are more affluent have other concerns that occupy them. There will always be plenty to occupy you but no matter what your situation is, you can take some time for reevaluation and seeing the overview.

Sometimes you become ill when you need time apart. It may be the only way that you will stop being so occupied with the details of your life. The problem with that is that you might then become occupied with being ill. But after a while, there is only so much that you can do: you have seen the doctor, slept, watched *Days of Our Lives*, and eaten as much as you want. Finally, you might take time to look, and if you look, perhaps you will see and understand.

Transcendence does not remove you from the realities of the world; it enlightens them. Perhaps it is necessary to appear to move away from the world to find the distance that gives perspective vision, but the point in doing this is not to deny the world.

If you say, "My life is terrible in every way. I have ruined everything. Nothing is good. Everything is going from bad to worse," you are not yet seeing objectively. The same is true if you say, after a quick glance, "Oh, everything's all right." The common use of correctional lenses is a symbol of the widespread lack of spiritual vision. We are not criticizing the use of such lenses, but spiritually, many people do not want to see, especially themselves.

If you are not accustomed to taking a hard look in the mirror, it may be daunting, even traumatic, because you will probably see many things you would like to change. But the purpose of looking is not to judge, not to make up a report card to take home to mommy and daddy; it is to give you information—that is all. If you see something that you do not like and this distresses you, remember that it was there yesterday, too, when you did not know about it, and perhaps you were perfectly happy at that time. Now that you see it, you do not need to plunge into depression over this new knowledge. If you are to be an artist "sculpting" your life, you have to be able to see where your sculpture is now so you can decide where to put the chisel next and how deep to go. The goal is to create something of beauty.

You might assume that you know all about yourself because you went to someone with a couch who explained it to you. This can be helpful, but what do *you* see? Someone else looked and told you what he saw; this may give you starting points, but what do you see? No matter how accurate the other person's appraisal is, if you do not see it, it does not do you any good. And what if he is wrong? You will never know for sure unless you self-validate.

You constantly receive other people's appraisals of you and what you do. You receive them from those with whom you work, members of your family, and so forth. Some "reviews" are good, some are mixed, and some are poor. Look at what is said and see if you see it. If you do not, at least at this time, allow the other person to see what she sees, and leave it behind.

Those who are overly influenced by the criticisms of others are usually those who have not looked at themselves, so they lack firsthand knowledge of their strengths and weaknesses. From your earliest days, you were evaluated by others. Your parents told you when you were good and when you were not, in their opinion. All throughout your schooling you were evaluated by your teachers, principals, and other students. Children are especially vulnerable to the evaluations of others because they are not yet fully capable of forming their own. But as an adult, you can look and see for yourself.

On the other hand, if you do not have an excessive attachment to being "right," you can receive criticisms from others with grace, learning from those you find valid. On your own, you might not have thought of them, so you can be thankful, even if the criticisms are judgmental rather than loving.

Anybody can set up a metaphysical program: "For enlightenment, drink this Kool-Aid." Are there guidelines for knowing when somebody is saying something valid, and when you are being sold a load of organically grown ...— well, you know?

You have to look and see, and then validate it for yourself, if it seems worth pursuing. If there were simple guidelines, or if there were somehow a truthful source of evaluation for every belief system being purveyed, they would still not be that useful to you. To discover what approaches are right for you, which might be different than for another person, you need to work your eyes and brain, and then see what your own experience is.

What happens when you disagree with your teacher? Sometimes I wonder if I'm resisting a truth that could serve me. I don't want to judge him, but I don't want to deny myself either. I'm not certain whether this relationship is still valuable for me.

If you disagree, you disagree. Part of your agreement with your teachers should be the right to disagree. A true teacher will have no problem with that. Someone who cannot tolerate sincere disagreement usually does not have that much to offer. A mature teacher/student relationship is one of equals. It is not like a parent/child relationship, in which the student is helpless and dependent on his teacher for knowledge and insight. Your teacher has as much to gain from your relationship as you do. If you withhold your perceptions from him, you may be doing him a disservice, depriving him of an opportunity to learn. He may be incorrect or incomplete in his views, or unclear in his communication with you. So do not passively accept what does not seem right for you.

If you speak with him about it and undergo honest self-examination, and do not see resistance in yourself, all you can do is stay open. It is unwise to assume that disagreement is resistance, although it can be.

To discern whether he has more to offer you as a teacher, step back a little and look. Take your time. You could try having less involvement with him for a while and see if you feel drawn back into more, or if life brings you another teacher. However, sometimes you need to teach others in order to better internalize what you received before you are ready for your next teacher.

I've looked at my life and, although there are nice parts to it, even those parts have negative undertones.

You are perceiving the mixed nature of human experience.

Let's give a simple example: Perhaps you basically like your house. You're especially thankful for the low rent and the convenient location, but it has high utility bills, and the neighborhood is a little noisy, so you are having a mixed experience. You probably cannot do much about the neighborhood, but perhaps you can have the house better insulated, reducing your utility bills and raising your satisfaction with it.

It is not necessary to have everything in your life exactly the way you want it to be; that is virtually impossible, anyway. But by identifying the things that you would like to change and beginning to take whatever steps you can to change them, you move in the direction of increased satisfaction. That movement is satisfying in and of itself.

You are in an in-between state. You are becoming aware of your feelings of dissatisfaction, but you have not yet completed identifying them. There can be immense release in just identifying them. Sometimes that requires you to see some unpleasant things about yourself, which may be why you have not yet done it. That is all right, too. When you are ready, you will.

You move a step at a time, as you are able, toward clarity in your life. Each person is on a journey toward greater clarity. If you are stuck in one area, work on another area where you can have some movement. When you come back to the first area, you might find greater ease in working with it.

How do you come to a place of transcendence when you're in the midst of a fury?

Take your time in responding. If you are not yet ready to say something that feels right to you, be silent. Stay as calm as you can. It is a wonderful opportunity to become more awake to the moment. Most people go on automatic pilot at this time and regurgitate what has been present with them in the past. If it is inappropriate, it sets up a negative pattern for the future.

It is easier to be transcendent in difficult circumstances if you practice in the less intense ones. You can also prepare for potentially difficult circumstances by being as clear about them as possible before going into them. If you do not find transcendence in a particular situation but learn from your experience, you will be better equipped to find transcendence in future situations.

21 ❈ INTEGRATION THROUGH THE HEART

The heart is an organ that receives blood from all parts of the body and then pumps it back. It is a neutral place of coming together and dispersing. Other organs, by contrast, have more specialized, local functions. It is similar to the difference between a meeting hall that can be rented by anybody, and a factory where screws are manufactured.

Like the physical heart, the spiritual heart is neutral. It provides a coming together place for the totality of your being. It is like a round table at which all your aspects can "sit down" together and come to greater synthesis.

Not only that: it allows you to connect directly with the Tao through your essence. The Tao is the core aspect of the universe from which everything dimensional springs. It is what is before there are stars, planets, and souls. Since the Tao encompasses everything, including you, it is logical that you should be able to connect directly with it. The Tao is the source of love, and the heart is often thought of as the seat of love, which is also logical. Red hearts are used on Valentine's Day, for example. A loving heart gives unconditional acceptance, respect, and kindness. In the heart, the different elements of self can soften, begin to hear and learn from one another, and blend.

If you confuse your emotions, which are immediate, feeling reactions to circumstances, with your heart, and you follow your emotions thinking that you are following your heart, you will likely make errors. We are not disparaging emotions. They are as vital an aspect of your being as your heart. But the function of emotion is not the same as that of the heart.

Suppose that you are angry at someone. You might think, "Well, my heart says that I should throw dishes at him. I'm going to follow my heart no matter what." It is wise to follow your heart, but that is probably following a transient emotion, not your heart. If you do that, you will probably not act in accordance with the highest good, whereas following your heart does produce the highest possible good. Sometimes it is appropriate to express anger in a visceral way. However, when an impulse comes only from a small part of yourself, you do not yet know whether it is appropriate. Only by bringing it into your heart and letting your whole self function can you come to your wisdom. Your wisdom springs from your whole self.

Often those who are more intellectually inclined try to replace the heart with the intellect rather than with the emotions. They try to come to resolution strictly through thought. This does not bring genuine synthesis, and resolutions on this basis are inadequate. Intellectual process has a place in heart function, as does emotional process; it cannot be one-sided, however.

Your connection with your essence is what allows integration in the heart to occur. Your essence is the part of you with the largest overview. However, it does not dictate either; it is a participant in the process along with the other parts of you.

You receive your thoughts and feelings into your heart through listening. Giving them space to interact together, they can change and integrate, resulting in integrity. When something has integrity, it is sound, worthy, and functioning well.

Sometimes people try to hammer out agreements or solutions among themselves. They may even sit at a round table, which signifies that everyone is equal, and each voice counts. Yet if everyone does not bring openness and flexibility, there will be limited success. Similarly, for integration to occur, your thoughts and feelings need to be open and flexible.

When you ask your heart something, you are setting in motion a process by which the various parts of yourself can gather and put together the wisdom you already possess in pieces, so to speak. If you are functioning merely at the level of intellectual perception, you have theory, not wisdom. Wisdom comes only after all the parts of yourself have democratically had their say. If you leave out a piece of your own knowing, your perceptions will, to that degree, be incomplete.

When people are mulling over situations, especially unpleasant ones, they often settle for incomplete integration, and therefore incomplete understanding. Maybe it is not comfortable for them to work all the way through the process, so they jump to conclusions. You can know when you have allowed your heart to process through to completion by the warmth and light that comes forth from it. You might say that when the meeting is adjourned, there is clarity. The light from your essence and, ultimately, the Tao can come forth. There is a sense of comfort, ease, and love. When your heart has done its job, there is no self-recrimination, nor is there recrimination toward others. There is merely understanding. True understanding sets the heart free, free to be that connection to the Tao. Love, in the sense of unconditional acceptance, is of the Tao. The Tao accepts and lovingly supports the entire universe completely without imposing on it to make it be some other way. The same is true of a person who has allowed complete integration to occur in his heart.

What are the different parts of yourself that can come together in the heart?

Your essence, intellect, emotions, and body often have different points of view. Emotions themselves are frequently in conflict with one another, as are thoughts, and even different parts of your body: your sore foot wants to stay still, while your shoulders want to move. You could also look at the parts of self in terms of your subpersonalities,, such as your "good child," "bad child," "nurturing parent," "critical parent." Any parts of yourself that are not in agreement can find integration in your heart.

Let's illustrate resolving a conflict between two emotions. Suppose, for example, that after an interchange with someone, you feel confused. Part of you feels angry because of something he said, and part of you feels remorse for something you said. Your anger might want to repress your remorse to justify itself, and vice versa. Instead, you bring them together in your heart and listen to both feelings with a loving attitude and an openness to the truth, seeing each of their validity. You realize that you had good reason for saying what you did, and also that you did not express yourself as appropriately as you might have. You see how you could have better handled the situation, and what you might say to him to properly complete your interchange. You might, for example, both apologize for what you said and appropriately tell him what angered you about what he said. In addition, if you discover that your reaction was aggravated by unresolved past issues, you can take steps to resolve them so that you can handle similar future situations with greater skill. After completing this process, you have released both your anger and remorse, and you have clarity about what happened.

Sometimes it takes courage to honestly face yourself and stay with the process of integration until it is complete, but there is much reward in so doing.

MEDITATION

Take a moment and listen to your heart. See if you can let the Tao and your essence bring forth in it an atmosphere of love and safety in which the integration of your being can take place.

22 ✺ ACCEPTANCE AND TAKING ACTION

Letting go, flowing, acceptance, and so forth, are important principles, but sometimes, in seeking to apply them, people misinterpret them and become too passive. The question arises: when do you act to change things, and when do you go with the flow, as they say?

To make an analogy, a boat may go with the prevailing currents, floating leisurely, or may change directions. There is a time for both. A skillful boatman uses what is happening to the greatest benefit. He knows the wind, the water, and the boat, and how to use them properly so that the movement over the water is as graceful and smooth as possible. He neither passively floats along all the time, nor does he direct all the time. He knows where he is going and, by being balanced in his approach, gets there in the optimal and easiest way. An unskilled boatman resists the winds when he should be going with them, and vice versa. He may try to impose his predetermined course rather than acting out of sensitivity to changing conditions. His actions may lead to seasickness, running aground, hitting rocks, or capsizing.

Balance is the key to success in living. To change analogies, if you are cooking a stew, too much salt is as bad as not enough. People like to make rules to obviate the need to make choices. One form of rules is a recipe: always add three-quarters of a tablespoon of salt. But a skilled cook knows that the seasonings must be adjusted according to taste.

The reason that flowing and letting go is so emphasized in New Age teachings is that the majority of people, particularly those in the West, are at the other extreme. The typical attitude is that everything has to be coerced into shape. In order to come to balance, you might for a time become quite passive, to learn what that is like. After a while you might find that things are not working in your life as well as you might wish. You might then go back to coercing, but hopefully, you will eventually find the balance.

There are some steps that can help in knowing when to act and when to wait or go with what is in motion. The first is to determine what is and is not within your power to change. If you do not wish to create karma, you cannot infringe upon the choices of other people. However, you can make suggestions and relate your own experience.

Let's give an example here. Suppose that you have a teenage son who is taking drugs, and it concerns you, naturally. If you are of a persuasion that says, "Let go and go with the flow," you might do nothing other than pray or hope that another source intervenes. There is a saying that "God helps those who help themselves." If you are unwilling to take any action, there probably is not a whole lot that others will be able or even willing to do to assist you in changing the situation. On the other hand, it is ineffective, maybe even counterproductive and inappropriate, to impose stern restrictions on your son: "You are not going out for six months!" or something like that. It will not stop him from taking drugs; it will merely cause him to become more secretive. In a situation like this, thinking about what actions are truly open to you might require some professional assistance. You might join a Twelve Step group and get help from them. You might go to a drug clinic and find out what is available in terms of treatment. You might read books as to the causes of drug addiction. Perhaps your most significant resource is your son himself. You might start listening much more carefully to what he says and observing what he does, seeking to learn more about him. Maybe you do not know him well enough. You would be wise to draw him out and see what is happening with him, being genuinely interested in him as a person. Maybe you have been neglecting this.

Once you know what is available to you to do and what is not, you can begin to seek guidance as to which of your options are the most appropriate in this particular

ACCEPTANCE AND TAKING ACTION

circumstance. Guidance may come from your essence, your spirit guides and/or teachers, trusted friends, professionals in the field—or you may find that you just know, if you give it enough time, what your next step is. Perhaps you feel that inviting your son to go with you for counseling to talk about the problem with no strings attached would be the next step. Once an appropriate step is taken, that is the time to let go and go with the flow, having no expectations of what your son does with the counseling, having no requirement that things work out a certain way, giving him unconditional acceptance, whatever decision he makes.

When the counseling concludes, if he chooses to continue with drugs, then you start from the beginning. You have a new situation to size up, because you have already taken a step. You must now decide what the next step will be. It is rather like exercising: tension, relaxation; tension, relaxation. When you move any muscle in your body, you contract and then release. If there is only contraction (action), you will get very tight. If there is only release (letting go), you will not move.

If there is truly nothing you can do to change a situation, acceptance, including accepting the right of others to make their choices, is wise; the alternative is wasting your energy and becoming frustrated, like pushing against a wall. If you find that it is too painful for you to be around, then you may have to separate yourself from it. You may feel sad, but you will not be in inner conflict if you know that you did what you could.

If someone transgresses against you and you have no recourse, accepting that allows you to at least take action internally, if not externally, to improve your experience of the situation. However, make certain that you indeed have no recourse.

Many people complain that the problems of the world are too great. After all, what can one person do? There is no one on earth who is more than one person. Some people have a wider influence than others, but if each person were to do what he could, the world would rapidly change. If you are deeply concerned about world hunger, for example, and cannot leave your present situation to work with Africans, there are things you can do right where you are. You can organize local programs to help the hungry, or volunteer for one if there is already one in operation. You can also donate money to organizations that help feed the hungry.

Wanting to do something and not doing it creates friction within you. Think about those things that concern you and decide if they are something that you wish to do something about. If so, make a plan and follow it. If not, then be honest with yourself that it is not something that you wish to deal with and put it out of your mind. If it keeps coming back to you, then maybe you need to consider it further.

Some people, although they may feel bad about those starving, say that it is the choice of those starving to be born into that situation: "It is their lesson, and therefore others should not interfere." However, their situation is not separate from yours. It may be your lesson to feed the hungry. They are a part of your situation and you are a part of theirs. You may choose or not choose to take any particular action, but it is inappropriate to rationalize inaction with spiritual principles.

You can accept things you are working to change. For instance, you can accept your body as it is while working to make it more fit. Acceptance is being at peace with things as they are. It is the starting point for change, whether internal or external.

23 ☸ OPENING TO WHOLENESS

You are not merely who you are in this life. You are the whole of you. Who you are in this life is but a tiny fragment of that whole.

Your essence could be said to be like a sun, and each planet revolving around it is like one of your reincarnational personalities. Although each planet has an individual identity, it also has an identity as part of the solar system. The solar system is present at each point within it. Just as each solar system has a magnetic field that characterizes everything in it as well as what emanates beyond it, you essence's field characterizes you and how you impact others in your life.

One of the purposes of a spiritual teaching is to assist you to open to the fullness of yourself so that you can more and more come to know yourself as being the solar system, not just the planet. Nothing we could say in words would be enough to trigger that opening, but words can help you to be aware of a potential experience.

MEDITATION

Be aware for a moment of the top of your head. Feel it opening. You might visualize a sunroof opening. You are assisted by many who are not physical. They are pleased to assist you in opening to the largeness of yourself. Feel their presence, and the exquisite sensation of opening to your wholeness.

Solar systems are themselves parts of galaxies and so forth. Where does wholeness stop? The answer, of course, is that it does not. However, particularly on the physical plane, it is necessary to practice opening to wholeness in manageable chunks, so we will stick with the solar system.

If your wholeness is incomprehensibly vast, then what is it that holds all its parts in place? For that matter, what holds solar systems together? You know about magnetism and such, but what causes the magnetism to operate?

This mysterious quantity has been called love. The same word is used for less cosmic purposes, not without reason. Love is the source of magnetic attraction among people as well. However, there are greater and lesser realizations of this force. Each experience of this force is valid, but the greater or deeper and more accurate the experience of it, the more satisfying and fulfilling it is.

If the highest degree of love on a scale of 1 to 100 is 100, it is not practical to think that you can go from 13 to 100 at once. Eventually you will, but if you go from 13 to 17, that would be a major and uplifting change.

Some people fear that if they let go to oneness, they will become colorless, just a drop of water identical to every other drop of water in the ocean. That would be boring for the Tao. There are actually infinite qualities in the universe, and although there is one whole, your place in that whole is unique. No one else can manifest what you individually can.

Experiencing wholeness is a lot more fun than experiencing blocked wholeness. Those are really the only two choices. However, it is not an either/or choice. Instead, there is a continuum from total openness to almost total blockedness. (That is not a word, but perhaps you will allow us to use it.)

The spiritual path might be described as opening to wholeness. Wholeness does not homogenize; it connects. You are interested in opening to wholeness—otherwise, you would not be reading these words. Opening to wholeness is opening to something that is beyond the world you know. That is an adventure, is it not? Opening to wholeness is not boring; it is exciting. You never know what you will find. Opening to wholeness does not occur merely at spiritual gatherings, in meditation, or through other spiritual practices. Everything that you do ultimately helps you open to wholeness, some things more directly and more easily than others. Whenever you are creative, you are opening to wholeness. Whenever you learn something new, you are opening to wholeness. When you go beyond what you have known in a relationship, you are opening to wholeness.

Breathing is a good analogy here. Someone whose breathing is shallow is partaking of only a small amount of the atmosphere that is available to him, whereas someone who breathes deeply is connecting with a greater portion of it. Through breathing, you connect with the entire atmosphere, although obviously you do not breathe all the air around the planet, at least not at once. The goal is not to breathe all the planet's air at once, but to completely unblock your breathing so that it is free.

One of the issues that comes up around the subject of opening is safety. You may feel a little unsure whether you can safely open to your wholeness—you might lose yourself or be hurt. The experience of greater wholeness is never forced on you. It is simply available to you when you feel ready to receive it. However, it is always safe to open to it. Not only that, it feels good!

In spite of the fact that there is work involved, the spiritual path is one of enjoyment and pleasure. What would the point of it be if it made you bored and miserable? The work you do pays off, just as in any other field of endeavor. It requires discipline, but it does not have to be onerous. The key is being relaxed and fluid.

Since our past lives are part of our wholeness, how deeply should we delve into them in order to be whole?

While most people on the spiritual path can benefit from some past-life work, you do not necessarily have to work with your past lives in order to open to your wholeness. Who you have been is present in who you are now. If you know who you are now, you also know who you have been. Of course, knowing who you have been can enhance your knowledge of who you are now. Both work together. But it is your choice how you approach knowing yourself.

How much opening to wholeness is done consciously? Do you do more of it on unconscious levels?

Your conscious and unconscious levels of self work together. When you consciously open, you catalyze the process of unconscious opening. You cannot fully open just from your conscious level, but the work you do consciously allows you to open more unconsciously than if the whole process were unconscious. One thing you can do to open to your wholeness consciously is to keep relaxing and sensing the infusion of light through the top of your head, as in the earlier meditation, or in any other way that reminds you to do it.

As you continue to open to your wholeness, you find that you are part of a larger and larger whole. The ultimate statement of wholeness is "I am." Finally, there is nothing that you are not.

Part VI

PRESENT IN THE NOW

24 ☀ SILENCE—THE GREAT MOTHER

[*After silence.*]

There are those who worship in this way, sitting together in complete silence. There is validity to such an approach. Many are not comfortable with silence. Behind everything is silence. Between spoken words is silence. Otherwise, the words would be unintelligible. Silence is, in a sense, the Great Mother. Out of her comes all creation. The womb is pretty much a silent place, other than the ever-present beating of the heart.

There is no listening without inner silence. Without listening, there is no true receiving. Noise promotes a feeling of being cut off from others. Silence engenders a sense of connection. As you listen, hear the silence as well as the words. The silence explains the words.

25 ❀ RELEASING FEAR OF THE CURRENT INSTANT

Every instant is unique, never to be repeated. Although there are infinite instants where this one came from, all you need to consider is this one, rather than being overly wrapped up in instants coming or regretting those past. The significance of the instant you are living cannot be overemphasized.

People's minds are often preoccupied with everything but the current instant, largely because of fear. Noise can be a distraction from fear, whether internal, from busy minds, or external, from such things as blaring radios. When your mind is racing, you might ask yourself what you are afraid of. In fact, it is useful to explore how great a role fear has in your life in general. You may not be phobic; you may consider yourself a normal person, and you probably are. But if you dig beneath the surface, you will likely find myriad fears running your life.

Fear is the opposite of love. To the degree fear rules you, love does not. Fear manifests in many ways, such as through anxiety, tension, worry, and even concern sometimes. Sometimes people put on fronts, acting as if they are not worried, for instance. This is also a manifestation of fear— if there were no fear, there would be no effort to put up a front. People who use substances such as alcohol or drugs to relax are often ruled by fear. It is so uncomfortable that they try to escape its sensation through these substances.

In the current instant, there is no fear unless there is an actual danger present. Fear is a useful mechanism. A little fear in the presence of a true threat can help you mobilize your resources to keep yourself protected. We are not suggesting a complete elimination of fear. But fear that is related to a true threat in the current instant is quite different from subconscious fear controlling you. Maybe you have tried to get your mind to quiet down unsuccessfully. Here is an example of fear controlling you: it seems to have more power over your mind than you do. However, although your mind may temporarily become noisier rather than quieter as your resistance to the current instant asserts itself, if you keep letting go, your mind will become quiet.

Sometimes people mesmerize themselves in front of a television set to escape the noise of their minds without coming into the instant they are living. They substitute the chatter of the television set for their internal chatter. If all television and radio broadcasts ceased for, say, more than a week, many people would be crawling up the walls, because they are so used to using them as a way of keeping themselves out of the current instant.

Pain and discomfort, and even pleasure, are distractions from the current instant when people react to their feelings rather than actually feeling them. One would think that pleasure would be an incentive to come into the current instant, but many people cannot become sufficiently relaxed to enjoy their bodies without blotting out their consciousness with drugs or alcohol. When that is the case, their enjoyment of their bodies is not a vivid experience of the instant they are living; their bodies are experiencing pleasure, but they are not fully with the experience.

People's deepest fear is of facing themselves. When noise is no longer distracting you, all that is left is you. You might have to acknowledge that you feel you are bad, boring, or empty. That might seem devastating, but only the truth can make you free, and the truth can only be seen in the instant you are living. If you truly love yourself, you enjoy facing yourself, just as when you are in love with someone else, you enjoy spending time with her. If you are to learn to love yourself, you must deal with your fear of facing yourself.

Some people are good at concentrating. Usually, that involves forcing their minds to focus on a particular task, using effort to keep other things out. It is good to be able to do that sometimes. But such effort would probably not be

RELEASING FEAR OF THE CURRENT INSTANT

necessary if there was no fear of the instant being lived. It would be easy to pay attention to what is now.

What are some of the benefits of living in the current instant?

If you're right there, alert, aware and ready, you're more poised and able to act effectively.

You experience more deeply.

What are some of the benefits of experiencing more deeply?

You're more alive and satisfied.

You also have more power. When you come into clear focus in the present, it is like focusing a slide you are projecting on a screen. When it is just right, it is quite different from when it is even a little off. It is so much more pleasing when it is in focus. When you are focused in the present, much more power can come forth from your inner self. To make another analogy, it is like the difference between cutting something with a sharp knife and a dull one.

The entire universe exists in the current instant. If you are in the current instant, you have the potential of tapping into the power of the universe, to the extent that you can handle power. When you are not in the current instant, it is as if you are running off batteries that had been charged in some other current instant.

Another benefit is being in control, whereas if you are somewhere else, you're not.

Outside of the now, fear—and whatever that fear is attached to—controls you. In the now, you have a chance to exert mastery, which allows power to manifest.

Continuing the analogy of a slide projector, you can focus it, but if the slide itself is faulty, you'll still have a poor picture. How can you make your slide clear?

The slides you project on the world are your beliefs. To clarify them, be willing to see the truth about everything, especially the truth about yourself. The truth is of the present. If you are willing to see the truth, it is easier for you to be in the present. You might say the truth sets you free to be in the present.

There are exercises you can do to help you to be in the present. As you drive, try to notice everything, taking it all in without editorial comment. Notice the bumper stickers and license plates. Notice the precise shapes of the trees and buildings. See if you can notice things you never noticed before.

As you become more advanced at this, you can try radiant vision. See yourself as being that slide projector, sending out light and healing energy through your eyes to everything you look at, such as the car ahead of you and its occupants.

This exercise can be extended to all of the senses. Listen to everything there is to hear. Sit in a quiet room and hear the sounds that are still there, such as the hum of the refrigerator, crickets, cars going by, or just your heart beating. Take it all in without judgment. If you are petting your cat, feel the texture of his fur. Notice if it feels different at the nape than on the back, for example. Feel the fabric of the clothes you are wearing. You might have someone test you to see if you can identify articles of clothing based on their feel.

Try eating your food in complete silence with no distractions, no reading, no thinking about other things, and see if you can taste every morsel of your food. A more advanced approach to this would be to bless every morsel of your food as it goes down, which would add to your health, among other things. Be certain to chew it well, not mechanically, but actually tasting it as you chew.

Notice the smells of the leaves in autumn, perceiving if maple leaves smell different from oak leaves, and so forth.

Extending this to other people, really listen when you are listening, taking in every word. Notice their body language, tone of voice, and posture. Do not judge or feel that you have to immediately analyze what it all means. After a while, you will tend to know a lot about others from your observation without having had to analyze in great detail. Listen fully without interrupting, and then, when you are talking, listen to yourself fully. Hear what you are saying. Hear how you are saying it. Notice how it feels to say what you are saying.

Notice how it feels to do what you are doing. When you walk, experience your feet as they touch the ground. Do your feet feel connected to the earth as you walk? What does the wind feel like as it moves across your face?

There is a tendency to make judgments about what is perceived: "I shouldn't feel this way" or "That person is wrong." No one is wrong, but like a wine connoisseur, a connoisseur of life needs to be able to make true discernments. How can you discern accurately if you do not even have the capacity to perceive what is actually there?

You are on the physical plane to live on the physical plane, not merely to survive as long as you can. A life is drudgery not so much because of the activities of that life but because of the way the life is approached. Most experience their lives as if they were anesthetized. Have you ever found it difficult to get through to someone when trying to communicate something quite simple? Has anyone ever found it hard to get through to you? Perhaps one's communication skills need improving, but sometimes there is the psychological equivalent of a thick layer of cotton batting in the way. When this is eliminated, there can be a vast increase in one's sense of aliveness.

The greatest benefit of living in the present is an increase in the experience of love. Love is the first force of the universe. Many people claim that they are seeking love. What they usually mean is they are seeking someone to love them, to take care of them, to fulfill their needs, sexual or otherwise. If a person is to truly find love, he must come to where love is. Love is in the instant you are living.

Living in the now, there's a lot of comfort because it's perfect. It's just the way it is.

This has much to do with acceptance. If you accept things as they are, it is much easier to be in the present, and much more comfortable.

Why do people so often seek, without enjoying the present?

We have wondered that ourselves. True seeking leads to enjoyment. Those who are seeking falsely do not wish to actually find what they seek. Their attachment is to the seeking itself. They would not know what to do if they found it. The ideal is to enjoy each instant of your life, which you tend to do if you are living in it. In the instant you are living, there can be a constant expansion of enjoyment, as you receive more and more of what you seek.

MEDITATION

Imagine a pinpoint of light in front of your third eye. Ask it how you can learn to live in the current instant, and receive the answer. Feel this light coming inside your head. Experience it fully and receive its energy, absorbing it as if you were a sponge.

It is good to be in the instant you are living. When you yield to it, you begin to receive its gifts. You begin to enjoy life—both the seeking and the finding.

26 ❊ ENGAGING WITH THE UNIQUENESS OF EACH MOMENT

It is sometimes said at spiritual gatherings that the right people are present whether the group is large or small. There is truth in this. Each gathering that is for a higher purpose draws to it specific people for particular reasons. This is not to say that everyone who agrees to be present on an essence level attends, or that everyone who attends had agreed to on that level. But each gathering broadcasts a vibratory signal made up of its particular potentials that draws those who can complement them. How they will be developed once all the ingredients are put together to cook in the pot, so to speak, is not known ahead of time. The ingredients include each person attending, those participating who are not physical, and the uniqueness of that moment in time.

The uniqueness of any moment can never be duplicated. No two moments are precisely the same. The more skillfully you address the uniqueness of the moment, the higher the quality of your results. Some moments present challenges that are more difficult than others, but the outcome reflects how adeptly you address whatever those challenges are. The more you practice, the more expertise you develop.

No combination of factors is intrinsically bad or good, just as no mountain is bad or good, yet some are more difficult to climb than others. Mountain climbers like that because it gives them opportunities to develop their skills further. Some mountain climbers tackle mountains that are too steep for their abilities. Similarly, there are souls who create circumstances that are substantially more difficult than they are capable of handling. At the other extreme, there are mountain climbers who always stay with the easier mountains, and souls who choose to limit their challenges to a specific kind or level of difficulty. In time, however, most learn to set up their lives with just about the right degree of challenge to support growth without it being overwhelming. There is a saying that people are never given more than they can handle. As indicated, this is not always true, but it usually is.

The perception that you cannot handle a challenge often arises from panic. Panic may be triggered when you remember a prior experience that was painful and that you did not handle skillfully. However, it is not necessarily true that you cannot handle the present situation. If you panic when confronted with a difficult challenge, it is helpful to detach from it and calm your mind. It is all right that you do not immediately know how you are going to deal with it; if you did, it would not be a challenge, and challenges are part of the game. It is sometimes necessary to try some solutions that do not work before you find a solution that does. These false starts are called mistakes; you do not learn without making some. The more detached and awake you are, the fewer mistakes you will likely need to make in order to find an approach that works. Nevertheless, if it is a substantial challenge, you will probably need to make some mistakes.

There is nothing wrong with mistakes. When people look at nature, they see perfection, incredible beauty and synchronicity. However, the Tao has had enormous practice in making planets; if this were the first planet, it would probably not be so impressive.

Whatever they are, your abilities relative to your challenges are fine—the point of the game is not primarily results, but to use and increase whatever abilities you have. In spiritual circles, people like to compare how young or old various souls are, often looking down on those who are younger. There are planets where, by comparison, the most exalted soul on Earth would appear backward. On the other hand, the lowliest soul on Earth in terms of evolution could be seen as being quite advanced from another perspective. In any task you undertake, there are usually those who are less advanced than you are and those who are more advanced.

ENGAGING WITH THE UNIQUENESS OF EACH MOMENT

You can always find someone to feel superior or inferior to, no matter what your level is. In any field, even the greatest person as acknowledged by the reigning authorities is eclipsed by what he could be. This is one reason it is a waste of time to compare yourself to others. Everyone is perfect where he is, and everyone in the universe must start from where he is—no exceptions. If you are self-deprecating, you might discount where you are, and if you are arrogant, you might exalt where you are. But where you are does not lie. You know where you are by observing your life.

Another reason that comparisons are a waste of time is that no two situations are the same. Everyone in every moment of existence is dealing with unique circumstances; therefore, how can comparisons be made? If you are an artist, you cannot properly compare yourself to Picasso. You are not the same people; you are not in the same circumstances. Picasso obviously had more skill than you do, but he could not do the work that you can do.

A great lesson of the physical plane is choice. Since every situation is unique, there are no real precedents for making choices. Paradoxically, every choice you make gives you skill in making future choices. But skill in making choices is not based merely on what you have done before. You can learn from what you have done before, but making good choices requires that you engage with the uniqueness of the moment. The more you do this, the greater your skill becomes. Your perception of the uniqueness of the moment grows deeper and more accurate.

Observing without preconceptions, without jumping to conclusions, is a key to accurately perceiving what is going on. Asking questions when there are things you do not understand can also add to your clarity. It takes a certain amount of time to fully comprehend a new challenge. Eventually, all the pieces of perception come together.

Our task when being channeled is to accurately identify the nature of the moment and to skillfully address it. We do not decide ahead of time what we are going to say. If we did, our listeners would probably still enjoy it, but it would not be the same as engaging with the uniqueness of the moment. We choose what we say not just to communicate ideas but to initiate the healing of consciousness. To do this, we must identify and work with the consciousness that is present.

One of the challenges of the physical plane is to stay awake. You live in a dense atmosphere and it is easy to go through life sleepwalking, or on automatic pilot, as they say. How often do you relate to others in a habitual fashion? When you do, you are missing out on the unique configuration of that moment. It will never come again. You can only experience essence contact, which is the source of all joy, in the present.

You might think that it is a lot of trouble to interface with every single present moment. It does require retraining, which is not without effort, but the effort is more than repaid. Race car drivers, when competing, are under pressure to interface with the uniqueness of each moment. If they do not, they could find themselves on the astral plane very quickly! Why do people like to race cars? Why is it thrilling? Partly because of the experience of being intensely with things exactly as they are and addressing them as skillfully as possible. In such a situation, one never knows what to expect. In fact, expectations can be fatal. Therefore, they are mostly eliminated.

Those who race cars might say that they feel powerful. They probably assume that this sense of power comes from the fact that they are driving their cars at high speeds. That is part of it. But when a person is interacting with the present moment consciously, there is a sense of power, which does not manifest when one is on automatic pilot.

Stress could be defined as a challenge you must see accurately and interface with in a new way in order to handle it. Any change is stressful. Why? Because if you keep handling the changed situation in the way you did before the change occurred, you will not be successful. Stress requires you to be present and bring your resources to bear. If there was no stress, there would be little growth.

As mentioned, you can have more stress than you are ready to handle. Even the most skillful race car driver would not want to be driving on the track several hours each day. There are times to rest. But as you gain skill, you can handle more challenge with less effort and wear and tear. This is the primary value of spiritual studies. Truly spiritual people, rather than being impractical, can handle the challenges of life more easily. Otherwise, what is the point of the studies?

The purpose of exercise is to stress your body in such a way that its ability to handle stress is expanded. If formerly you could climb only one flight of stairs without being winded, and you practiced so that you can now climb twenty without being winded, five flights of stairs do not seem like much.

Taking things one at a time reduces stress. Suppose that you have a houseful of furniture to move to another location. You would not attempt to get under the house and lift the entire house in order to move its contents. You would move each article one at a time. Some people are overstressed because they are trying to handle a large problem as a whole instead of just taking each step.

Even if you are fully engaged in the present moment and marshaling all your resources to find the most skillful way of responding to it, you will make mistakes. Again, mistakes are no big deal. If you make one, it will be part of the situation you will be dealing with in another moment. If you continue to engage with your moments, you can easily handle your errors.

As you grow in your skill in meeting challenges, you find greater enjoyment of life. Those who are only capable of playing scales on the piano, although they may enjoy it, do not experience the fulfillment of those who are able to play sonatas.

EXERCISE

List challenges you are now able to handle that you were not able to handle a few years ago. Also list challenges you still are not very skillful at handling. Review the second list later and note your progress.

The more you meet challenges, the easier it becomes to meet new challenges.

It is true that each person creates her own reality, but to change your reality in the direction you wish requires acknowledging things as they are and bringing your resources to bear upon them skillfully. You cannot create a workable new reality if you do not know what your present reality is.

It seems that most of the time, we're out of touch with our essence.

You are automatically aligned with your essence when you engage with the uniqueness of the moment. Your essence is present in the moment. If you are asleep to the moment, you are by definition out of alignment with your essence. If you want your essence to be a greater presence in your life, the first thing to do is acknowledge the moment as it is. Having done this, you can deliberately open wider to the presence of your essence. The more you pay attention in the moment, the wider the opening is for your essence to come forth. Consciously inviting your essence to permeate your life helps you open further.

I tend to panic when I do not know what is going on or cannot affect what is happening, especially in unfamiliar situations. How can I handle this?

When a challenge arises, in most cases you have some time

to work with, so you do not need to feel driven to react immediately. Deep breathing and affirmations can be helpful. You might remind yourself that you are probably not going to die as a result of this challenge, and if you do, that is not so bad either—you are eternal! That will help you detach and engage with the moment so you can discern what is happening and better decide how you are going to handle it. If you are impatient and react before you are prepared, this will add to your confusion. See yourself as playing a game. Race car drivers usually see what they do as play, not work, yet they probably work more intensely than most people ever do in terms of marshaling their full resources.

This is a time of accelerating change for humanity, a time when rigid precedents will not work, if they ever did. If you are flexible in meeting these changes, you can accommodate them relatively easily.

MEDITATION

Experience this moment exactly as it is. Observe everything about it, staying as free from preconceptions as you can. Know that everything about this unique confluence of factors is perfect, and that your abilities to engage with them, whatever they are, are perfect as well.

Again, notice this moment and see if it has changed.

Viewed from outside it, the present moment may seem to be racing by—here and gone, here and gone—but when you are engaged with it, it is motionless. It is the still place from which motion, whether it appears fast or slow, emanates. It is empty, yet includes all possibilities. It is the clear place from which all colors spring. From the present moment, you can paint your reality with your beautiful, unique colors. As you do, you grow naturally and joyfully.

BACK MATTER

ABOUT THE AUTHOR

SHEPHERD HOODWIN has been channeling since 1986. He also does intuitive readings, mediumship, past-life regression, healing, counseling, and channeling coaching (teaching others to channel). He has conducted workshops on the Michael teachings throughout the United States and Europe.

Shepherd is a graduate of the University of Oregon. He lives in Laguna Niguel, California.

https://shepherdhoodwin.com

TWITTER:
@shepherdh
@EnlightenNitwit

FACEBOOK:
https://www.facebook.com/shepherd.hoodwin
https://www.facebook.com/shepherd.hoodwin.author/
https://www.facebook.com/JourneyOfYourSoul/
https://www.facebook.com/EnlightenmentforNitwits/

shepherdhoodwin@gmail.com

Summerjoy Press
99 Pearl
Laguna Niguel CA 92677-4818

GLOSSARY

Agape: A state of unconditional love for everything. This is considered the highest goal.

Astral plane: Where we go between lifetimes and when we are finished with the physical plane.

Causal plane: The next plane after the astral. Michael's plane of creation.

Essence: Soul, or higher self, in distinction to the outer personality, or lower self.

False personality: False ego, the part of self motivated by fear.

Physical plane: The densest of the seven planes, where we presently reside.

Soul: Essence, or higher self, in distinction to the outer personality, or lower self.

Tao: The All That Is. Usually refers to the dimensionless ground of being rather than to its expression in the seven planes of creation of the manifest universe. Michael normally uses the word *Tao* in place of God (depending on the beliefs of those listening) because God is usually personified and tends to connote something hierarchical and judgmental. They sometimes also use the word *God* to signify the overall consciousness of the manifest universe.

OTHER BOOKS BY SHEPHERD HOODWIN

Available at https://shepherdhoodwin.com/book/

All Is Choice

Few realize how profound, multi-faceted, and far-reaching the concept of choice is in our spiritual growth. This short book explores topics such as what is and is not our right to choose, our power as creators and the limits of our reality creation, how consciousness expands, and much more.

Being in the World

This insightful book explores practical spirituality. Topics include aging, karma, time, and religion.

Compassion for Evil
A Metaphysical View

Compassion for Evil explores the nature of evil from the soul's point of view, and how we can skillfully deal with it as lightworkers.

Embracing What Is
Spiritual Keys to Happiness

This book is an abridged version of *Happiness and the Michael Teachings*, without technical Michael teachings terminology. A free version is available at Smashwords.com.

Energy Literacy
How to Perceive and Take Charge of Your Spiritual Well-Being

Energy Literacy is an introduction to how to perceive our energy field and release negativity. Topics include chakras, contracts, vows, cording, entities, implants, psychic attack, earthbound souls, soul retrieval, and more.

Enlightenment for Nitwits
The Complete Guide

This hilarious metaphysical/self-help humor collection will appeal to Oprah and Dave Barry fans as well as those with more esoteric interests. In a style reminiscent of comedian Steven Wright, it's full of wry one-liners along with longer, hilariously mind-bending pieces on a wide range of subjects, tied together by the idea of clueless humans trying to find enlightenment.

"I love *Enlightenment for Nitwits*! It is the funniest book I have read in several decades. If laughter leads to enlightenment, it will certainly do it. Nothing—thank God—is sacred in this delightful spoof on life in general."
—C. Norman Shealy, M.D., author of *Life Beyond 100*

Happiness and the Michael Teachings
Learning to Embrace What Is

Happiness is the ultimate goal of every spiritual teaching. Here we explore several principles of what the Michael teachings refer to as growing through joy.

Healing the Gut
A Crib Sheet for Eliminating SIBO

This short book offers tips for those with digestive problems and related diseases, focusing on the Specific Carbohydrate Diet.

Journey of Your Soul
A Channel Explores the Michael Teachings

This is the most in-depth discussion of the Michael teachings to date. It may also be the first analytical study of channeling written by a channel. It has forewords by John Friedlander, co-author of *Psychic Psychology*, and Jon Klimo, author of *Channeling: Investigations on Receiving Information from Paranormal Sources*. Klimo writes, "*Journey of Your Soul* may well be the best (Michael) book of them all due to its clarity, thoroughness, and detail, and thanks to the fact that the author, an exceptionally clear-headed Michael channel himself, brings real integrity and authenticity to our understanding of Michael in particular and to the channeling process in general."

Loving from Your Soul
Creating Powerful Relationships

This inspiring, transformative book explores the nature of love itself as well as practical matters of relationships. One reader wrote, "There are phrases that are so inspiring that I wrote them down to refer to when I need them. I am looking forward to reading this book again and again."

Meditations for Self-Discovery
Guided Journeys for Communicating with Your Inner Self

This is a beautiful collection of forty-five vivid, often pastoral, guided imagery meditations channeled from Shepherd's essence. There are many meditation recordings available, but this is one of the first collections of meditations in book form that can be read to oneself or others. Teachers and group leaders would find it particularly useful.

Opening to Healing

This uplifting book explores the spiritual aspect of healing.

Unconditional Love in Politics
Or Have You Hugged a Republican/Democrat Today?

Is unconditional love in politics an oxymoron? Thus far, it's been a rare commodity if it's ever been there. This book explores what you can do about it, as well as why both right and left have useful parts to play in our evolution, the factors that influence a person's tilt to the right or left, and what unconditional love might look like in this sphere.

Why We're Attracted
Spiritual, Psychological and Physical Elements That Draw Us to Others

Just why are we attracted to some people and not to others? This book explores a multitude of factors on three levels: spiritual, psychological, and physical. Topics include agreements, life path, soul chemistry, male/female energy ratio, celibacy, body-type attraction, sexual orientation, monogamy, and polyfidelity.

REVIEWS

Another great and uplifting book, with gems on every page.

Growing Through Joy is an easy and enjoyable read, and will apply to nearly anyone's life. In fact, there were many instances in this book where I felt like it was talking directly to me. And maybe it was! The lessons taught are easy to understand and apply to daily life. The central theme of the book is how to remain centered and achieve personal growth by working through challenging issues using a different and less painful perspective than most people employ. Overall, another great book from Shepherd Hoodwin.

Clear, concise, comprehensive. *Growing Through Joy* is an exceptional road map to well-being. For spiritual students, this work confirms, affirms, and refines what we have learned.

Be aware of the temptation to read this work quickly and superficially. Much of what is here may seem familiar and even obvious. A more accurate assessment of its authenticity is evoked with a gradual reading over an extended period of time.

Growing through joy is really possible! With the wisdom and loving compassion characteristic of his work, Shepherd Hoodwin brings Michael through with clarity and power. *Growing Through Joy* is a wonderful addition to any spiritual library for its practical instruction on experiencing joy even when enduring the inevitable pain of life. It contains methods for avoiding the suffering and self-judgment that contracts us and compounds the pain. Like all of his books, it is rich and dense with information that stimulates our own experience of inner truth. Using the tools provided is an excellent way to achieve more spiritual presence and balance through every challenge of life. As usual, the teachings of the Michael entity resonate with love, compassion, humor, patience, and a call to presence as who we really are. Shepherd expresses this consistently and powerfully through all his channeled works, and this latest offering is no exception.

I gained a great deal from this book.

All of Shepherd Hoodwin's books are wonderful. As soon as I start reading them, I connect with a pure and loving energy that is very moving and healing. Want spiritual insights, growth, and healing? This might be what you're looking for. Highly recommended!

Printed in Great Britain
by Amazon